PARTY
of ONE

PARTY
of ONE

Arnold Schwarzenegger and the
Rise of the Independent Voter

Daniel Weintraub

Foreword by Michael Barone

PoliPointPress

Party of One: Arnold Schwarzenegger and the Rise of the Independent Voter
By Daniel Weintraub
Copyright © 2007 Daniel Weintraub

Production management: BookMatters
Book design: BookMatters
Cover design: Jeff Kenyon

Library of Congress Cataloging-in-Publication Data

Weintraub, Daniel, 1960–.
　Party of one : Arnold Schwarzenegger and the rise of the independent voter / Daniel Weintraub ; foreword by Michael Barone.

　　p.　cm.
Includes bibliographical references and index.
ISBN 0-9794822-2-4 (alk. paper)
1. Schwarzenegger, Arnold. 2. Governors—California—Biography. 3. California—Politics and government—1951– I. Title.
　F866.4.S38W45　2007
　979.4'054092–dc22　　　　　　　　2007042117

Printed in the United States of America

Published by:
PoliPointPress, LLC
P.O. Box 3008
Sausalito, CA 94966-3008
(415) 339-4100
www.p3books.com

Distributed by Ingram Publisher Services

For Janice, Max, and Abe

Contents

Foreword

California is different. Not since 1860 has a single state been home to such a large percentage of the nation's population. Most Americans live in flat or slightly rolling land with steady year-round rainfall or snow and changing seasons. Most Californians live in huge metropolitan areas in the margins between the ocean and mountains or spreading out into the desert, where rainfall is seasonal and natural vegetation sparse. Most Americans live in the state or metro area where they grew up. Californians live in a state that has grown from 6 million just before World War II to 38 million today.

California politics is different as well. Nearly a century ago it was one of the pioneers in adopting initiative, referendum, and recall, allowing the voters to make decisions over the heads of elected politicians. The intention was to circumvent the lobbying prowess of the railroads and other business interests. But as government grew, ballot propositions became a weapon of the populist right even more than the populist left, as voters froze property taxes in 1978 and subjected legislators to term limits in 1990.

In the past two decades the state government in Sacramento seemed impervious to the sweeping changes in California life—the vast flow of immigration from Mexico and Asia, the economic churning caused by the surge and then swift decline of major industries. Defense contractors boomed during the Reagan buildup of the 1980s, then tanked with the end of the Cold War in the early 1990s. Silicon Valley boomed with the Internet revolution of the late 1990s, then tanked as the NASDAQ fell 70 percent from its peak in March 2000. Meanwhile, state legislators passed redistricting plans that made each party's seats impervious to competition while the state elected governors—George Deukmejian, Pete Wilson, Gray Davis—with bland enough images that each could go unrecognized at almost any of California's hundreds of shopping malls.

As the twenty-first century began, state government proceeded without scrutiny by California's television stations and with the good reporting in the state's newspapers going largely unread by an electorate accustomed to getting its news on the tube or through the net. Only when dysfunction became tangible did people start to notice. That was when the lights and the air conditioning went off in 2001, as the electricity deregulation system passed by a bipartisan majority of legislators malfunctioned. There was also a fiscal malfunction. Revenues from those earning over $1 million soared from 1995 to 2000 from $3 billion to $15 billion, and from 1998 to 2000 state spending rose from $57 billion to $80 billion. Gray Davis, reelected by a reduced margin in 2002, tripled the car tax. A conservative activist took out papers to force a special election in which voters would decide whether to recall Davis and at the same time vote on who would succeed him if he were recalled.

Enter Arnold Schwarzenegger. The Austrian immigrant had already had two successful careers, as a bodybuilder and a movie star. He had married Maria Shriver, niece of John F. Kennedy and daughter of Sargent and Eunice Shriver. After finishing the promotion of his last movie, *Terminator 3*, he went on Jay Leno's *Tonight Show* and announced his candidacy. He was elected governor in 2003, and California politics has not been the same since.

In *Party of One*, Daniel Weintraub tells this story. I first encountered Weintraub by reading his blog and his column for the *Sacra-*

mento Bee; I ran into him only once, on the campaign trail outside an elementary school in San Bernardino, where Schwarzenegger made one of his brief, carefully scripted and staged appearances designed to produce great TV footage. I was impressed by Weintraub's reporting, which showed not only an understanding of politics but also an appreciation of public policy and the workings of government that you don't find in most political coverage.

From my perspective in Washington, D.C., Schwarzenegger's political course has been filled with twists and turns. He worked with the Democratic Legislature in 2004, then in 2005 sponsored four ballot measures intended to undermine the political power of the Democrats and their chief backers, the public employees unions. After he lost at the ballot box, he fired his Republican chief of staff and hired a Democrat, once again worked with the Legislature in 2006, and was resoundingly reelected. In 2007 he stepped forward with an ambitious program to reduce carbon emissions, joining forces with other governors and with allies as distant as Prime Minister Tony Blair. He appeared on the cover of *Time*, with New York Mayor Michael Bloomberg as the latter ostentatiously dallied with the idea of running for president as an independent.

Daniel Weintraub sees Schwarzenegger in great detail and subtle nuance. Working with different-minded advisers and choosing from an eclectic array of options has been Schwarzenegger's modus operandi in all three of his careers. He has the conviction that he can achieve any goal if he wills it strongly enough. "His visions are sweeping, his projects huge," Weintraub writes. "His ideology hop-scotches across the political battlefield, plucking positions from the right, left, and center, sometimes melding all three. He wants results, and though he does not always get them, his obvious yearning to move forward, try new things, and take risks endears him to a new kind of voter who wants government to work for a change." But Weintraub is not uncritical about the results. He brings his knowledge of the workings of government and the unglamorous details of the state budget to his narrative. And he brings also a large measure of fair-mindedness. He is intrigued with Schwarzenegger and curious about how the governor thinks and interacts with other people. But he is not dazzled.

Will California and Arnold Schwarzenegger turn out to be a harbinger of our political future, as California has so often been in the past? We certainly will not see another bodybuilder and actor become governor in a recall election ever again. Arnold Schwarzenegger is different. But perhaps California is not so different from the rest of America as it has seemed over the last decade or so. Perhaps Arnold-style politics—a call to consensus that attracts independent voters and independent-minded Democrats and Republicans—will prevail elsewhere or in a presidential election. In any case, one out of eight of us Americans lives in California. Eight out of eight of us have a stake in how government works there. In the pages that follow, Daniel Weintraub tells not only the story of an extraordinary politician but also the story of how the nation's largest state government is and isn't working. And he leaves us eager to find out what comes next.

September 2007   *Michael Barone*
Senior writer, *U.S. News & World Report*
Resident fellow, American Enterprise Institute

Introduction

The first time I sat down privately with Arnold Schwarzenegger, shortly after he took office as governor, I was surprised at how grounded he was. He had been a superstar bodybuilder and a famous Hollywood actor. Now he was chief executive of the largest state in the country. Having watched him in action for several months, I expected something of a prima donna.

But as we shared lunch at Lucca, his newly favorite Sacramento dining spot, Schwarzenegger exhibited a trait I hadn't anticipated: humility. He wasn't exactly shy. But he didn't try to dominate the conversation. He seemed curious. He asked questions. And he didn't look the slightest bit bothered when Bonnie Reiss, his long-time friend and adviser, would sometimes jump in and finish his sentences.

What impressed me most was how he wanted to talk about more than just politics and government, even though these topics were then dominating his life. We talked in depth about the condition of the state he was now leading. But we also chatted about our wives, our families, our passions. And it was a genuine conversation. It stretched from the Valentine's Day gift he and his children were making for his wife, Maria Shriver, to the quality of the skiing at Lake Tahoe.

This might seem unremarkable if you are not a person who hangs around with politicians much of the time. But as a reporter who has covered California's Capitol for 20 years, including the tenure of four governors, I can say that it is rare indeed—especially for someone who has reached the pinnacle of power that the California governor's office represents. Most people who win that post have made it there by dedicating nearly every day of their lives, from a fairly young age, to climbing the political ladder. They are political junkies. They simply don't have much else to talk about.

Schwarzenegger's varied life experiences make him more than just a good conversation partner. They give him a surprisingly normal take on politics and policy. By "normal," I mean the kind of approach I see in my friends and family who are neither part of professional politics nor even active along the edges, just regular citizens with an interest in civic life who try to vote most of the time. These people might be registered to one political party or the other, but they don't define themselves that way. Most of them have a core ideology or at least a set of beliefs that shapes the way they view the world around them. But it is not something they cling to as if it were a Holy Writ. They're flexible. They're realistic. They sometimes change their minds as they learn more about a topic, or as the facts change. And that, in a nutshell, is Arnold Schwarzenegger.

For the past four years, I've watched Schwarzenegger do his job as closely as anyone. And I've watched with a special interest. Like Schwarzenegger, I am not wedded to the views of any one political party. I have been a registered Republican and a registered Democrat, and I am currently registered with no party at all. I consider myself to be a fiscal conservative with a bit of a libertarian streak. I believe in individual responsibility. When it comes to social policy, I think government should act only as a last resort, and mainly to ensure equal opportunity, not equal results. I am an old-school liberal, a live-and-let-live person who believes government should generally leave people alone to do their own thing.

And I am an environmental progressive, because when you blow soot into my lungs or dump toxins into my water, you are no longer just doing your own thing. You're messing with my life. As it turns out, these beliefs are a pretty good match for Schwarzenegger's.

I can also say with confidence that he and I are not all that different from many of our fellow Californians. Based on my experience covering politics and my 47 years as a native-born resident of the state, I think his views are in sync with those of a strong majority of California's voters and with those of the rest of the nation. This set of views, however, does not fit neatly into the dogma of one major political party or the other. And given the deeply partisan nature of organized politics today, and the way the political system is stacked to favor the partisans while marginalizing everybody else, Schwarzenegger is left stranded, nearly alone, in the middle.

As governor, he has been unable to rely on a consistent set of allies in the Capitol. Instead, he has built a series of constantly shifting alliances. On one issue he might scrape together a majority of his fellow Republicans and enough Democrats to get something done. More often, he has found himself in agreement with almost all of the Democrats in the Legislature and almost none of the Republicans.

It has been fascinating to observe, and not always satisfying. Despite our similar takes on life, I have been disappointed often with Schwarzenegger's performance. I think that he has done a terrible job on the biggest issue that prompted his election as governor: managing the state's budget. I also think that for much of his first two years in office, he was neither as bold nor as creative as he had the capacity to be. At first he adapted all too well to the Capitol culture he had so harshly criticized, and when he decided to confront it, he did so clumsily and with such poor execution that he offended both his friends and his foes and accomplished nothing. On important issues such as criminal justice and immigration reform, he for several years lacked the courage of his convictions, missing opportunities to educate the public and build consensus for sensible solutions. In a few crucial instances, he has failed to question his staff, or his instincts, aggressively enough. He has, in short, not lived up to his potential.

Schwarzenegger's strongest suit has been his willingness to tackle big, complicated issues that many politicians would rather avoid. From local government finance to infrastructure, prison reform, water policy, health insurance, and the environment, he has taken on problems that have been festering in California, and in the entire country, for years. If his solutions are imperfect, his enthusiasm cannot be denied. And his independence, not only from the political parties but even from many of the private interests that have contributed to his campaigns, is intriguing.

My goal in writing this book was to explain the origins of Schwarzenegger's governing style, to assess his record in office, and to explore the relevance of his career to the politics of the rest of the country and to the issues people care about in their everyday lives.

The book is divided into three sections. Part I details the development of Schwarzenegger's political philosophy from the time he came to the United States as a young man until he was elected governor and it explains how he makes decisions within the context of his bipartisan governing style. Part II traces his rollercoaster early years as governor, from his relatively successful first 12 months to the disastrous year that followed and his remarkable comeback, ending with his landslide reelection in 2006. Here the book examines how Schwarzenegger was one of the few Republicans in the country to succeed in one of the most Democratic years in a generation, and do so in a state dominated by Democrats. Part III examines the unfinished business of his second term; his ambitions to do big things on health care, prisons, education, and political reform; and his desire to spread his post-partisan gospel to every corner of the country. California has often been a trendsetter for the nation, and the problems Schwarzenegger is addressing today are likely to be on the national agenda tomorrow.

Could his movement spark a surge of independent politics in 2008? It seems likely that independent voters will play a greater role in that election than they have in the recent past, either through the existing parties or the candidacy of a third-party or in-dependent candidate. Polls show that as many as half of Americans favor the idea of building a new independent political party to field a credible candidate for president, and only a handful say they would not consider voting for an independent candidate in 2008. With that in mind, independent voters and independent-minded members of both major parties can learn much from Schwarz-enegger's successes and his failures about how solutions-oriented governing works in today's highly partisan political environment. But voters who prefer ideological purity to compromise might be alarmed by what they read here about how Schwarzenegger is try-ing to change the central dynamic that drives American politics.

I hope this book serves as a guide to readers of all political per-suasions who want to better understand the Schwarzenegger phe-nomenon, its effect on California, and its potential application to the rest of the nation.

Sacramento, California   *Daniel Weintraub*
August 2007

PART 1

RISE TO POWER

If the state of American politics in the first years of the twenty-first century was defined by anything, it was by the increasingly bitter relations among the major parties' lawmakers and executives. Beginning with the Clinton years at the end of the twentieth century and then picking up steam with the disputed election of George W. Bush in 2000, politics became more personal, its participants angrier. But in California, in 2003, just the reverse was happening. The historic recall election that brought down a Democratic governor seemed, on the surface, to be the ultimate partisan revenge play. But the result in the end was the election of Arnold Schwarzenegger, a Republican who appealed to independents and Democrats and whose own ideology fit into nobody's camp. Schwarzenegger governed by instinct, by anecdote, by gut, his decisions shaped by his life experience and by the eclectic group of advisers, paid and unpaid, with whom he surrounded himself. His first campaign, his election, and his move into the governor's office in the nation's most populous state all made for political theater like none the country had seen before.

ONE

Bootstraps

Arnold Schwarzenegger is the last person in the world you would expect to undergo a midlife transformation.

Born to a family of modest means in a small town in Austria but blessed with an abundance of ego and determination, Schwarzenegger left his native country as a young man to pursue his vision of the American Dream. He believed with the passion of the converted that anyone who worked hard and focused on his goals could make it in America. Not just make it—but make it big. Fame. Wealth. Adulation. A beautiful family.

And that is exactly what happened. By the time he was 50, Schwarzenegger had become the most famous bodybuilder in the world and then, arguably, the best-known actor in Hollywood. He was rich, with his own restaurant and a real estate empire to augment investments from his multimillion-dollar movie paydays. He married a woman—Maria Shriver—who was descended from a fairy tale American political family, the Kennedys. A successful television news personality herself, Shriver brought even more glamour to his life. She eventually bore him four handsome children, and the family lived on a compound in west Los Angeles, with cooks and maids to attend to their every need. They spent winter vacations skiing with wealthy friends in Idaho and traveled by private jet to summer on Cape Cod.

Given all that, Schwarzenegger might have lived out his life con-

vinced that his youthful assumptions were correct. Everything he
thought *could* happen *did* happen. Why should he doubt his world
view when his own experience proved its accuracy?

At first, he had no such doubts. As a new immigrant, barely old
enough to buy himself a beer, the beliefs of America's Democratic
Party reminded him of the socialism he had so disliked in Austria.
In the Republicans, he saw more respect for the individual, which
reflected his own beliefs about how life worked.

Schwarzenegger studied business in college and, feeding a
casual interest in economics, eventually became a devotee of
Milton Friedman, the country's foremost Libertarian philosopher.
Schwarzenegger read one of Friedman's books, *Free to Choose*,
loved it, and gave it to his friends. Its tracts dovetailed perfectly
with his own dislike of government and his belief that individual initiative was the key to success in life. He later met Friedman and
struck up a friendship. When the economist prepared a video series
based on his book, Schwarzenegger agreed to tape an introduction.

America, he said, was a place where you were "free to live your
own life, pursue your own goals, chase your own rainbow, without
the government breathing down your neck or standing on your
shoes."[1] As he became a citizen and took an interest in partisan politics, Schwarzenegger identified himself very much as a Republican.

"I would say that a lot of the things that I believed (were) based
on my own personal experience, and my own personal experience
was that I operate better if there is no safety net," he said. "I am
much more alert, and I'm much more aware that it's up to me, and
there is no one else there, and it creates a certain kind of an extra
energy and willingness to perform. And I always felt that that
worked well for me, and therefore that's the way it ought to be
with all human beings. And so, therefore, if anyone talked about,
you know, a safety net, or helping people, giving them money, welfare, or any of those kinds of things, (that) was to me something
that is very, very counterproductive. No one should ever feel that

there is anything out there, or anyone there to help. You've got to be on your own, and that will make people perform."[2]

That was before Schwarzenegger met the Shrivers—not just Maria, but also her parents, Sargent Shriver and Eunice Kennedy Shriver, a sister of the late President John F. Kennedy. Schwarzenegger never embraced the big-government liberalism of Maria's uncle, Senator Edward Kennedy of Massachusetts. But Schwarzenegger was affected by the intense belief in public service he saw in Sargent and Eunice Shriver. Eunice was the founder and moving force behind the Special Olympics, a worldwide charity dedicated to improving the lives of the developmentally disabled. Sargent Shriver was the first director of the Peace Corps, part of the call to service that inspired so many to believe in JFK's "New Frontier."

Harris Wofford, a longtime friend and associate of the Kennedys and the Shrivers, was at the Shriver compound the first time Schwarzenegger visited in the summer of 1977, shortly after he met Maria and her siblings at a charity tennis tournament in New York. Killing time before a family outing, Wofford found himself walking on the beach with the 30-year-old bodybuilder and discussing his life's story.

"He said, 'If you will something with your full will, everything you've got in you, you are likely to get it,'" Wofford recalled 30 years later.[3] Schwarzenegger told Wofford that he had willed himself into being the strongest boy in his town, then the world's best bodybuilder. Now he was going to will himself to becoming a world-famous actor.

"It was a fun time," Wofford said. "He was provocative, and he can tell a story well. He got me to tell my story. And then he asked, 'What would you most like to do? If you could have any kind of job, what would you most like to do?'"

It might seem an odd question for a young bodybuilder to ask a man such as Wofford, who was 50 at the time and had been a Notre Dame law professor, a special assistant to President Kennedy, and one of the founders, with Sargent Shriver, of the Peace Corps. He was then president of Bryn Mawr College in Philadelphia. But Wofford took the bait. He told Schwarzenegger he had always wanted to be a United States senator.

"He said, 'If you will it, you're going to make it.'" Fourteen years later, Wofford was sworn in as a senator from Pennsylvania.

Wofford never forgot that conversation, or the young man's unshakable belief in the power of the human spirit. He remembered it as he witnessed Schwarzenegger's transformation from an inward-looking individualist to someone who had a more layered view of the world.

"He is a bright, resilient, ambitious guy who has, I think, been deeply influenced by the whole of the Kennedy and Shriver families," Wofford said.

Over the years, at dinner at the Shrivers' Maryland home, or sailing off Hyannis Port—wherever they were—Schwarzenegger heard story after story of public service. He couldn't help but absorb the Shrivers's passion. Others said that Sargent Shriver was like a father figure to Schwarzenegger, who had lost his own dad when he was a young man. The elder Shriver was serious about public service, but he also loved life, loved a good time, and was famous for his hearty laughter. Ever the sunny optimist himself, Schwarzenegger took to him instantly.

"When we went on trips, it was always like, 'Let's go on a fun trip to the Bahamas on a vacation,'" Schwarzenegger said recently.[4] "But then, of course, instead of lying on the beach it was visiting this school and how they teach those poor children, or visiting this Special Olympics place where kids are training with nothing, and just barely making it. Or meeting this priest—because they're very religious—and talking to this priest about his work that they are doing. So that all to me was, even though I felt like it was a little bit over the top, I said, 'Well, that's what the family does, is that.' But I felt that every time when I left the East Coast, or their home, or

Hyannis Port, or going on a trip, or when they came out to California, I was always inspired by that."

The contrast was sharp with Schwarzenegger's own pursuits, first as a bodybuilder and later as an actor.

"Coming from a sport—well, a sport, first of all, and then the profession where you only think about yourself—you know, for me the beginning was all about, okay, I'm struggling in Austria, so I will find a way to work on myself to get to accomplish all my goals. So it was about me. . . .The acting was about me, and how can I make a million dollars a movie. That's what Clint Eastwood made at that time. That was my goal. I had to make what Clint Eastwood made, and what Charles Bronson made, and what Warren Beatty made, and what Marlon Brando made. Those were the guys that were the million-dollar players. So I said, 'I'm going to do this. No matter what it takes, I'm going to make a million dollars a movie.' Of course, then I make the million dollars a movie, then they made five million dollars. I was immediately pissed off."

Schwarzenegger has by no means shed his ego. He still, for instance, decorates his home and offices with images of himself in action. His entire life has been, in one way or another, a celebration of self. But he slowly began to appreciate that not everyone could do what he did. Not everyone was born with the advantages he had.

He remembers Sargent Shriver giving a speech to a group of graduating college seniors, telling them to think about more than just themselves. "Don't look in the mirror and just look at yourself," Schwarzenegger said, paraphrasing his father-in-law. "Get rid of the mirror, look beyond, and you will see millions of people that need your help."

As he looked outward from his Brentwood mansion, Schwarzenegger saw beyond the affluence of his neighbors to the poverty over the hill. He saw children raised without fathers, by drug-addicted mothers who left them to roam the streets after school or to skip school altogether. He saw gangs drawing these young people, especially boys, into their criminal networks. Even children who tried to stay straight met intimidation on the streets and, often, neglect in the public schools.

"I used to go around saying, 'Everybody should pull himself up by his own bootstraps, just like I did,'" Schwarzenegger said in a speech in 2001, two years before he ran for governor of California. "What I learned about this country is this: Not everybody has boots."[5]

As he began to rethink his views, Schwarzenegger found himself with ideas that contradicted Friedman's small-government take on the world, not to mention those of the Republican Party to which he belonged. Schwarzenegger's focus was on America's children, especially those growing up without the advantages he had enjoyed.

"Most of them don't get the motivation," Schwarzenegger said. "Instead they hear, 'You're a loser. You'll never make it out of the barrio or the ghetto. You'll never get out.'"

"The more I saw, the more I realized I'd been wrong when I thought the American Dream was available to everyone. Because even though it is the land of opportunity for me and the majority of Americans, millions are left behind. It's not a level playing field for them."

Eunice Shriver recruited Schwarzenegger to become an "international coach" for the Special Olympics, exposing him to the plight of disabled people around the world. Later, she pushed the first President George Bush to appoint Schwarzenegger as chairman of the President's Council on Physical Fitness and Sports, a post that led him to visit schools around the country. Following his mother-in-law's example, he adopted a fledgling Los Angeles after-school program known as the Inner-City Games after the 1992 Los Angeles riots, and he started a foundation that would take the idea to cities across the nation. By 2003, the foundation said it was providing after-school, weekend, and summer programs for 200,000 children in more than 400 locations. It also formed the basis for his successful California ballot initiative, Proposition 49 in 2002, which expanded public funding for after-school programs. Schwarzenegger used that measure as a political prop to introduce himself to the voters as a person serious about public policy. But it was also consistent with his own interests and with his belief that government had an important role to play in improving the lives of disadvantaged children.

Schwarzenegger's experience with the Inner-City Games and his role as chairman of the fitness council brought him into the schools and into the streets, and what he saw sometimes shocked him. Once, he says, in Georgia, he was pitching his program to the governor, who took him to neighborhoods where, at 9 a.m., many of the children were still in bed instead of in school. There was no one home to tell them to get up and get going, no one to push them or hold them accountable.

"He said, 'You're talking about getting physical fitness instructors here, and for kids to have daily physical fitness activities . . . I am trying to just wake up the kids and get them to school.' And he said, 'Do you understand what I'm dealing with? So when you try to hustle me to get more money into physical education,' he says, 'that's what my interest is.' So it was just interesting to see all this. And every governor had their own little things.

"So what I'm saying is, that when you're out there and you see that, then you realize that that kid may be—and I'm not a psychologist or a psychiatrist—may be not having the same kind of foundation where he has the confidence that he will be great one day, that he could lead something one day, that he will have an impact on the world one day. That's how I grew up, you know? I mean, I grew up with that, I had people around me always telling me that I'm great, and that I can make it, and I got the support system. . . . They pushed and pushed and pushed you. 'You can do better. You can be great, but you have to push more.' So it was that."

Schwarzenegger thus began to question his long-held beliefs. "These kids that I see roaming around on the streets at 3:00 in the afternoon when we close the doors of the school and the gates of the playgrounds and all this, and now they're out on the street, and no parent waiting there, and now they get into trouble. . . . So now all of a sudden you say, 'Well, then, someone else has to take over.' Well, who is that? That's the schools. So all of a sudden I'm contradicting myself, because in my own mind now you have a battle from one side to the other where you say, 'Wait a minute. Your philosophy is that government shouldn't, you know, be responsible for raising kids and being the nanny and doing all this.' And so all of a sudden you start to see a conflict in your own thinking, where certain philosophic things started falling apart. . . . So it was a lesson, that you can't really be stuck to just one belief, because things change."[6]

Over time, Schwarzenegger became more pragmatic. His Libertarian instincts still made him look first to individual initiative and responsibility, more so than most Democrats who run for political office. His own private foundation represented that tradition. But he was also more willing than most Republicans to support the use of government to create opportunity for the disadvantaged, and do other things that private markets weren't doing well on their own.

"I still believe government should ensure a fair start and fair competition for all," Schwarzenegger said in 2001, explaining his transformation. "It shouldn't rig the outcomes. I still believe in lower taxes—and the power of the free market. I still believe in controlling government spending. If it's a bad program, let's get rid of it. But I also believe that government is important—and should be in the business of educating our children, defending our people, ensuring public safety, advancing scientific and medical research, and more."[7]

This was two full years before he ran for governor, and five years before political pundits everywhere discovered his tendency to swing from left to right and back again. He does have that tendency. But he has had it for many years. It is a central part of his political DNA. It's not that he is a Republican one year, a Democrat the next, or a conservative one minute and a liberal the next. He is all of those things wrapped into one. All the time. What the public sees at any given moment is whichever side he happens to be stressing at that time, or whichever side his opponents on the left and right decide to shine the spotlight on.

In 1998, for example, Schwarzenegger condemned his fellow Republicans for impeaching President Bill Clinton after he lied in grand jury testimony about his extramarital affairs. Two years later, when Democrats held their national convention in Los Angeles, Schwarzenegger and Maria Shriver hosted a soiree that attracted some of the party's biggest stars. Yet later that same year, he supported George W. Bush for president.

As a politician, Schwarzenegger simply does not fit well into either major political party. He has developed positions on issues in a way that felt right to him, without regard to partisan implications. He is more comfortable as a Republican, and probably more successful there than he would have been as a Democrat. Although he might raise taxes for a specific purpose or support new regulations on business, he prefers less of both. He embraces capitalism, globalization, and growth with a gusto that most Democrats find difficult to sustain. He believes in tough criminal sentencing laws, including the death penalty. He favors standards, testing, and accountability in the schools, and he has been a strong supporter of public school choice. He is suspicious, to say the least, of public employee labor unions.

But many of his beliefs have more in common with Democrats than with Republicans, at least those Republicans who hold public office. He supports abortion rights, for instance, and civil unions for gays and lesbians. He has been a strong supporter of embryonic stem cell research. He is an ardent environmentalist. And he believes that government should play a bigger role in expanding access to health care.

On immigration, one of the most divisive issues of our time, Schwarzenegger has refused to choose sides. Instead, he has a foot in at least two camps. He is for securing the borders, unhappy with illegal immigration, and openly impatient with immigrants who do not embrace the United States, or the English language, as eagerly as he did. But he also is a big supporter of legal immigration and of providing some services to illegal immigrants, and he opposes proposals to send illegal immigrants home.

Because his views so often cross party lines, true believers on both sides have accused Schwarzenegger of lacking a core. And most of the time he does make decisions on a case-by-case basis, rather than applying a rigid ideological test. He will set aside principle to make progress on something he wants to accomplish. But if there is a thread that runs through his positions on most major issues, it is a focus on personal responsibility, individual freedom, tolerance, initiative, and equal opportunity. He also has a profoundly European sense that the government must think ahead, plan ahead, and build for the future, even though this sense sometimes collides with his belief in personal freedom.

This powerful combination of values, if ever harnessed in a single party instead of being split between Democrats and Republicans, would probably command a majority of American voters. These values almost certainly reflect the views of a majority of California voters. And they might even reflect the thinking of a majority of California Republicans, although that party's activists and formal structure are dominated by religious and fiscal conservatives, many of whom are suspicious of immigrants.

If Schwarzenegger could remake his chosen party in his image, it would be the dominant party in California, perhaps the nation. But the Democrats could also learn from him. With a little more focus on personal freedom and personal responsibility, with more respect for entrepreneurs and risk-takers, that party could also capture many voters who are now in the middle or loosely attached to the Republicans. Call them Schwarzenegger Republicans.

For now, at least in California, Schwarzenegger has the middle pretty much to himself. His success to date demonstrates that among the electorate, out there where people are not obsessed with politics or ideology but simply are living their lives, going to work, raising children, his centrist straddle strikes a chord. That is true even if, within the insular world of organized politics, and certainly within the Capitol, he often operates as a party of one.[8]

TWO

A State of Confusion

Standing on the stage in the ballroom of the Century Plaza Hotel in west Los Angeles, with red, white, and blue confetti raining down upon him, a dark suit draped perfectly over his sculpted body, and a smile as big as Yosemite Valley across his face, Arnold Schwarzenegger on Election Night 2003 looked every bit the celebrity candidate come to claim his prize. Many observers outside the state, and even some inside it, would attribute Schwarzenegger's stunning, almost overnight ascension to his fame, his money, and the tendency of Californians to embrace wacky politics. It seemed crazy. Direct democracy run amok.

It was all of that. But it was also much more.

To see the incongruity of it all, one had to look no farther than the crowded stage on which Schwarzenegger stood. It was filled not only with Hollywood stars but also with the extended family of his wife, Maria Shriver, most of them descended in one way or another from the Kennedys, a national Democratic Party dynasty and institution. And yet they were on that stage to celebrate a Republican's successful campaign to banish a Democratic governor who had not yet served a full year of his second term, who had committed no crime, no act of moral turpitude, not even a transgression against his party.

The recall election that begat Schwarzenegger was California at its best and its worst. It was an impulsive, impatient act by voters

21

swept up in the moment. It was also a cry of frustration. At a time
when California was leading the nation if not the world into the
New Economy, its government could not keep the lights on or the
budget balanced. Its once-famous freeways were pocked with pot-
holes and choked with traffic. Its public school students were per-
forming at a level on par with those of Mississippi and Louisiana.
Its prisons were overflowing with criminals. A higher percentage of
its residents were going without health insurance than any place
else in the country. Schwarzenegger, with his irrepressible optimism, his outsider's disdain for government, and his pledge to be a
bipartisan problem-solver, was the perfect vessel to carry that frustration to Sacramento and beyond.

Schwarzenegger was in the right place at the right time, an
avowed centrist who managed to ride the activism and money of
conservative Republicans to success. But to place his career as
governor and his potential effect on the nation in context, consider
that the story of the election that put him into office is the story of
California itself, of a destiny the place simply cannot shake. This is
a state built not by aristocrats, polished gentlemen, or religious pioneers, but by hardy individualists who came here to get rich quick
and live the good life. In a nation of immigrants, California has been
the final frontier, the end of the line, the western terminus for thousands and then millions fleeing persecution or prosecution or simply seeking a better life. Most of those early settlers lived hard and
died poor. But they left a legacy that grips the state to this day. It is
a state of instant gratification, of wanting something for nothing, of
enjoying the blessings of some of the most beautiful landscapes
and most hospitable weather anywhere, without, for the most part,
being willing to make the long-term investments necessary to sustain it. And it is a state whose politics have always been unpre-
dictable, because nothing is sacred here. No institution, no elite, no
inner circle has the standing to tell the people what to do and get
away with it.

While California is unique, it has also been the nation's edge state, a window into the future of the rest of the country. The revolt against property taxes that began there in 1978 eventually spread to other states and into national politics, propelling Ronald Reagan into the White House and making tax increases, which used to be just another government policy option, into something that most politicians were afraid to propose. Similarly, a backlash against immigration, and especially illegal immigration, hit California in 1994 at a time when the rest of the country hardly knew a problem existed. But by 2006 immigration was perhaps the top issue in America (although by then California had largely come to terms with it). The state practically invented environmentalism, and its early battle against air pollution became the model followed by the national government. So, too, might California's growing disdain for party politics—an attitude that Schwarzenegger has come to embody—soon be commonplace across the country.

The major parties have never been strong in California, in part because the state's residents have little respect for institutions of any kind. Political machines have never thrived there. If one begins to grow, it quickly becomes the object of derision and is likely to be smashed. Patronage is practiced in only limited form. Organized labor for many years was weak, and still is, by eastern standards, though it has lately made a political comeback by building on the foundation of the state's growing number of public employees. The fastest rising group of voters consists of those who refuse to register with any party. The parties, in fact, are an insiders' game. They are weak by design, and few real people connect with them or are involved with them in any meaningful way. California was the original do-your-own-thing state, a place that cherishes individual freedom. That mood extends to its politics.

It only made sense that direct democracy would flourish here. It began with Hiram Johnson, the early twentieth-century reformer, a local prosecutor who ran as a Progressive out to smash the power of the railroad barons and the Legislature they had corrupted. Johnson won the governor's office in 1910, and in a special election the next year, he persuaded voters to adopt the initiative, the referendum, and the recall as the ultimate check on the power of elected officials and aspiring party bosses. The ballot measure was used only sparingly for more than half a century, until 1978. It was in that year that voters, upset with ever-rising property taxes and a huge surplus in the state budget, passed a measure to slash their taxes and cap the growth of their annual assessments. Proposition 13 helped launch Reagan's successful candidacy for president and helped nurture a cottage industry of ballot initiative consultants, who stood at the ready to help anyone with a hot idea and a million bucks put their measure before the people.

Since then, the state has earned a reputation for governing by initiative. Some social critics suggest that the initiative has now empowered the very special interests it was designed to smash. There is some truth to this charge, but it doesn't tell the entire story. Some of the most controversial ballot measures passed in California in recent years were not sponsored by any economic interest group. They were ideologically based, playing to a public perception that the Legislature was not reflecting the will of the people. And their content is striking, considering California's reputation as a liberal bastion. In 1994, the voters passed a measure to limit public services to illegal immigrants, and another to lock up career criminals for life. In 1996, the state banned affirmative action. In 1998, bilingual education took its turn in the dock. Like Proposition 13, each was originally sponsored by outsiders who pushed the issue to the top of the public agenda despite indifference if not outright hostility from the political establishment. And in a state that was dominated by Democrats, each of these ballot measures passed by a wide margin despite being opposed by nearly every elected Democrat in the state. Those measures exposed a rift between the governed and their government. And they were, each in their own way, the parents of the recall movement that opened the door for Schwarzenegger.

California is the boom-and-bust state, and with every cycle, the booms seem to grow bigger and the busts more violent. It is a place that is both on the cutting edge of modernity and the closest thing America has to a Third World society. It is the first major state in which minorities constitute a majority, yet its politics remain in the grip of an aging white middle class. California is where millions live atop active earthquake faults that could, without a breath of notice, throw their homes or offices off their foundations, topple freeways, and send God knows how many people to their deaths. But while those quakes strike every 10 years or so, and everyone knows the most deadly and destructive one is still to come, no one except visitors and newcomers talks about the ever-present danger, as if ignoring the possibility will reduce its chances of happening.

The political fault lines that eventually brought Schwarzenegger to power began to shift ever so slightly on March 10, 2000, even if nobody noticed at the time. Governor Gray Davis spent that day in his Los Angeles office, as he did most Fridays, so he could finish up the week's work and retreat quickly to his West Hollywood condominium for the weekend.

Davis that day spoke to hundreds of enthusiastic elementary school teachers, commending them for participating in new training programs he'd created the year before to improve the teaching of reading in the state. He announced a couple of routine political patronage appointments, one to the state Unemployment Insurance Appeals Board and another to the Board of Pharmacy. And before going home, he issued a tersely written decision denying clemency to serial killer Darrell Keith Rich, sending the condemned man to his death.

If the busy governor noticed at all, he never said anything publicly about two events in the news that Friday. Both would transform what had been a fabulously successful beginning to his tenure as California's chief executive into a series of economic and political disasters that would shake the state and, ultimately, the nation. One was an uptick in the price of natural gas, the fuel that runs most of the power plants supplying California with electricity.[1] The other was a new record high on the technology-laden NASDAQ stock exchange.[2] That record came amid concerns that perhaps the most remarkable stock market rally in history was losing its momentum.

At the time, Davis had little reason to worry. California was admired worldwide as a shining example of the New Economy, a multi-ethnic, multi-lingual melting pot where entrepreneurs were busy building the future. It was America's Great Experiment, where Silicon Valley software writers toiled amid a state population teeming with immigrants from all over the world. It was also democratic capitalism at its best, with hundreds of thousands of jobs created not by big business but by start-ups and small firms growing larger. No longer was the state a captive to the military industrial complex or heavy industries such as automobiles and aerospace. Most of those jobs had been shed in the last recession, in the early 1990s, and replaced by something entirely new. General Motors and McDonnell Douglas were shutting down manufacturing plants. But Intel, Google, and Yahoo were hiring by the thousands. Between 1982 and 2002, 36 new companies had moved onto the list of the 40 largest firms in the Silicon Valley.[3] This incredible dynamism was working wonders on California's economy and its people. Poverty was on the decline, crime was down, and incomes were up across the board. And the wealth created by the inventors of new technology was creating new millionaires daily, fueling a tax windfall that would soon present Davis and state lawmakers with a $12 billion surplus.

That expansion of wealth was breathtaking. From 1995 through 2000, the number of California taxpayers reporting incomes of at

least $1 million quadrupled, from about 11,000 to more than 44,000.
And, thanks to California's progressive state income tax, those people were paying taxes like never before. In 1995, people earning $1
million or more paid about $3 billion in taxes to the state. Five
years later, the state's take from that group had soared to $15 bil-
lion. The taxes paid by this group of the super-rich, who accounted
for about one-quarter of 1 percent of all returns, represented fully
one-third of all the income tax collected in the state.[4]

The safekeeping of this bounty fell to Gray Davis, and it was a
job for which he should have been well suited. Davis could not
have been more different from Arnold Schwarzenegger. Cheap by
nature, he'd lived most of his life on a government salary. As a
young man he was the top aide to former governor Jerry Brown,
the flashy, creative, chief executive whose otherworldly ideas
earned him the nickname "Gov. Moonbeam." Unlike his mentor,
though, Davis was a deeply cautious man. He worshiped stability
above all, preferring incremental change to dramatic transformation. Governing, he once said, was like golf: you play it one shot at
a time. He began each day with a tofu smoothie and a workout and,
whenever possible, lunched on a turkey sandwich with a side of
broccoli. He wore the same color blue shirt to work day in and day
out. And he admonished his staff, sometimes in harsh terms, to
avoid ambushing him with unpleasant surprises.

Worried that the tax windfall from the dot-com boom might turn
out to be short-lived, Davis urged his more liberal Democratic colleagues in the Legislature to spend at least half the money on one-
time projects, so that they would avoid committing the state to
long-term spending that could not be sustained when the tax boom
subsided. But his pleas were ignored. The Democrats, back in
power after 16 years of Republican governors, had too many unful-
filled priorities to stop now. And the Republicans, unconcerned
about the potential long-term effects, had spending projects of their
own, along with a bushel of tax cut ideas that they were trying to

enact. Davis, always eager to avoid conflict, was happy that everyone could agree, even if, in this case, a little more conflict would
have been prudent.

And so the state dramatically increased spending on the public
schools, boosting teacher salaries to the highest in the nation and
reducing class size to help teachers in the primary grades deal with
the burgeoning immigrant population. The legislature expanded
health care for poor seniors and the working poor, adding more
than one million people to the rolls of the state's subsidized medical programs. Lawmakers cut state park fees, lowered state university tuition, and increased funding for police. State employees
got raises and expanded pension benefits. In just two years, state
spending soared from $57 billion to nearly $80 billion a year, even
as tax rates were reduced. Motorists saw their car tax slashed by
two-thirds, and parents with children got a bigger tax deduction.
California voters got their cake and ate it, too.

But it couldn't last. The natural gas price spike that gained
strength that March day turned out to be the precursor of an electricity crisis that soon crippled the state, forcing rolling power
blackouts, costing residents upward of $40 billion, bankrupting
one major California utility, and placing the other on the brink of
insolvency. The crisis was made possible by a flawed plan to restructure the electricity industry, forcing utilities to buy much of
their power in a volatile spot market just a day, or in some cases
minutes, before they needed it. That plan was exploited by private
power generators looking to make a fast buck, including Enron
Corp., the infamous Texas trading company that moved electricity
supplies in and out of the state in an effort to capitalize on short-
ages, or create artificial ones, and drive the price of an electron
sky-high.

The crisis was worsened by a painfully slow response from the
governor. His feebleness in the face of disaster was perhaps best
displayed on the December night in 2000 when he ventured down

the west steps of the Capitol to light the state Christmas tree. Once the ceremony ended, he ordered the lights turned off to set an example of conservation for his constituents to follow. It was a nice gesture but mostly meaningless. In reality, saving electricity at night, when there was a surplus, was not going to help much to keep the power running during the day, when supplies were tight. And even as Davis fiddled, his appointees on the Public Utilities Commission refused to give the utilities the authority they needed to buy long-term contracts for electricity that could have insulated the state's consumers from the worst of the price fluctuations.

The stock market peak on March 10, meanwhile, would be the last such peak before a collapse that eventually drained the NAS-DAQ index of 70 percent of its value and brought on a fiscal crisis that pushed the state deeply into debt, threatening its ability to pay its bills. With so much of the state's wealth, and the government's tax revenue, coming from the Silicon Valley, the dot-com bust bled the treasury. Once again, Davis was slow to react, and by the time he did, he was facing deficits as far as the eye could see. By July 2003, the state's bonds were rated just a hair above junk status.

With its energy industry in disarray, its economy wounded, and its treasury depleted, California's political process began to melt down. The ingredients were always there, lurking in 90-year-old Progressive era reforms and their holy trinity of citizen politics: the initiative, the referendum, and the recall.

Against the advice of elders in both parties, leaders in the business community, and most of the state's major newspapers, Ted Costa, a Republican gadfly from suburban Sacramento, launched a drive to recall the newly reelected Davis from office. With the help, first, of a ragtag band of followers and later, of money from a wealthy and conservative Southern California congressman, Darrell Issa, Costa and his allies spent the spring and summer of 2003 gathering the signatures of nearly two million California voters on petitions demanding a special election at which the governor could be recalled from office. No state since tiny North Dakota in 1921 had risen up against its governor. Yet here it was happening to a Democratic governor in California, arguably the most Democratic state in the nation, the party's bulwark against a conservative tide then running in favor of the Republican Party and its president.

Davis at first dismissed the recall as improbable, and then tried to prevent the activists from gathering signatures. His forces tried to disrupt the signature gathering and were encouraged to complain to store managers about the petition circulators out front. They circulated a petition in support of Davis that had no legal standing but was used as a way to pay petition circulators to drop the recall campaign. When that failed to slow the tsunami, Davis allies went to court to try to stop the signature count. His goal was to delay the election until March 2004, when it could be combined with the already scheduled presidential primary, in which Democrats were expected to vote in large numbers. But none of these tactics worked, and 1.4 million signatures were certified with plenty of time to force a special election in October.

Kevin Starr, the state's foremost historian, at first viewed the whole thing as a tawdry episode in power politics. But as the campaign progressed and captured the imagination of the electorate, Starr, a Davis appointee as the state's librarian, began to change his opinion.

"The culture of politics, the appropriations, the hearings, the budget proposals, the whole apparatus of California government is basically eighteenth century in origin," Starr said at the time. "It's become a self-perpetuating system, in both Republican and Democratic circles. On the other hand, people are getting information on a 24/7 basis. They're used to feedback. They're used to things being changed . . . Everything moves very rapidly, and people want that from their government as well.

"We are getting ready for the twenty-first century, getting ready for the destiny that history has given us," Starr said. "California is the epicenter of creativity in so many fields, and it has got to have a government equal to its creativity. The people understand that. They don't want to be bothered with the details. They just want it done."[5]

More than 130 Californians submitted their names and the $3,500 filing fee required to appear on the ballot should the voters decide to remove Davis. They included social commentator Arianna Huffington, former Olympics czar Peter Ueberroth, dot-com pioneer Garret Greuner (a founder of AskJeeves.com), former child actor Gary Coleman, porn star Mary Carey, and Angelyne, a woman famous for appearing on a Los Angeles billboard promoting nothing but herself. A number of more conventional politicians also joined the fray, including Bill Simon, the just-defeated Republican candidate for governor, and Tom McClintock, an articulate, conservative state senator. Cruz Bustamante, the state's lieutenant governor and the only prominent Democrat to run, was campaigning on an intriguing "no-yes" message: vote no on the recall, but in case Davis loses on that question, vote yes for Bustamante.

But none of them really ever stood a chance of winning, especially once Schwarzenegger decided to run. Conveniently enough, the petitions were certified and the election date set just as Schwarzenegger was wrapping up a promotional tour for his latest movie, *Terminator 3*. After sending signals that he would not run, Schwarzenegger appeared with his friend Jay Leno on NBC's *Tonight Show* and announced that he would be a candidate for governor after all. And why not? Schwarzenegger had been dabbling on the edge of politics for a decade and had contemplated running in 2002. He was almost certain to be a candidate for governor in 2006. But in a regular election, he would have needed to win a difficult Republican Party primary as a candidate supporting abortion rights, gay rights, gun control, and the environment. In this election, all the candidates ran together in one winner-take-all race. He could win with the votes of Democrats, independents,

Libertarians, and Greens, in addition to Republicans, and he didn't even need a majority.

"I know the people of California want better leadership, they want great leadership," Schwarzenegger said on the Leno show. "It doesn't matter if you're a Democrat or a Republican, if you're young or old. Everyone is welcome. As you know, I'm an immigrant. I came over here as an immigrant and what gave me the opportunities, what made me be able to be here today, is the open arms of Americans."

As the short campaign unfolded, Schwarzenegger focused relentlessly on three issues: the economy, the state's budget, and political reform. The economy, he said, was hemorrhaging jobs because taxes were too high and state regulations too much of a burden. He proposed—even in the face of the massive deficit—to cut the state's unpopular car tax, and he promised to overhaul the system for compensating workers who were injured on the job, a constant source of irritation to businesses large and small. He never offered a specific plan for balancing the budget, or even an outline, but promised instead to launch an audit and then quickly eliminate the deficit. And his entire campaign was built around the idea that "special interests" had taken control of the government. "Money goes in," he said, "favors go out, and the people lose." Carrying a broom to rallies around the state, he pledged to sweep the influence peddlers from the Capitol and restore the power to the people.

Behind the shallow sloganeering of his television commercials and his rallies, however, was a more sophisticated campaign and candidate. Schwarzenegger met with business leaders and local government officials, discussing in greater detail his plans for the state. He maneuvered adroitly to win the endorsement of key Republican Party officials even as one of his opponents—Senator McClintock—held his grip on the hearts and minds of conservative activists. And he managed to tap into Californians' latent optimism about their state and its future, promising that a shake-up in Sacramento could unleash the Golden State's potential to be great again. Conservative Republicans focused on his call for cutting taxes, while independents and many Democrats were attracted by his appeal to bipartisanship. He was both tough and compassionate on immigration (though most people only heard the tough side), progressive on the environment, and a big advocate for pushing control of government programs from the Capitol out to cities, counties, and school districts. Other than his lack of experience and just the idea of electing a former bodybuilder and action movie star to the governor's office—and late accusations about his misbehavior toward women—there wasn't much for voters to dislike.

Thanks to Schwarzenegger's celebrity, people were actually paying attention to the campaign for a change. In the years leading up to the recall, California politics were more and more becoming an insider's game of interest to candidates, pollsters, consultants, and political reporters, but few others. The election in 2002, when Davis won a second term, featured a record-low turnout for a governor's race. Barely 50 percent of registered voters, and hardly more than a third of all those eligible to vote, bothered to cast ballots. But the recall, and Schwarzenegger's campaign, changed all of that instantly. Polls showed that upward of 90 percent of California voters were following the race. The only campaign debate in which Schwarzenegger participated was broadcast around the world; in California, it was the most watched political event in history. On election day, 60 percent of voters turned out, a million more than had voted the year before, and the total might have been higher had not a federal court stepped in and temporarily blocked the election for two weeks as the campaign was coming down the stretch.

Schwarzenegger won in a landslide. The recall question passed by a vote of 55 percent to 45 percent, sending Davis into early retirement. And to replace him, voters chose Schwarzenegger over his closest rival, Lieutenant Governor Bustamante, by a margin of 49 percent to 32 percent. McClintock, the Republican state senator, finished third with 14 percent of the vote.

An exit poll showed that Schwarzenegger won 77 percent of the Republican vote, 46 percent of the independent vote, and 21 percent of the Democratic vote. He won 32 percent of the Latino vote, a respectable number for a Republican in California, plus 18 percent of the black vote, quite high for a Republican anywhere, and 46 percent of the Asian vote. He finished first among all age groups (doing best among ages 30–64), all education groups (doing best among those who completed some college but did not graduate), and all income groups, with his support generally rising with income. Twenty percent of voters who said they voted for Davis in the last election chose Schwarzenegger to replace him.

Standing on the stage at the Century Plaza as the results became clear, Schwarzenegger thanked the people of California, pronounced "Calee-for-nee-ah" in the accent of the chief-executive-to-be.

"From the time I came over to this country, you've opened up your arms to me," Schwarzenegger said. "You've received me. You've given me opportunities, endless amount of opportunities.

"I came here with absolutely nothing. And California has given me absolutely everything. And today, and today, California has given me the greatest gift of all. You've given me your trust by voting for me . . . And let me tell you something. I will do everything I can to live up to that trust. I will not fail you. I will not disappoint you. And I will not let you down."

The governor-elect promised to reach out to Republicans and Democrats, young and old, rich and poor, to those who supported him and those who did not. "For the people to win," he said, "politics as usual must lose."

It already had.

THREE

Five Hundred Push-Ups

If Arnold Schwarzenegger were preparing a new movie script, he says, he wouldn't hire just one screenwriter to get the job done. He would want a collection of writers with different interests and talents.

"Imagine how bad it would be if you have someone sitting there at the script meeting where you fine-tune the script, and you have only a writer sitting there that writes action," Schwarzenegger said.[1] "And he will now only tell you, 'No, no, you've got to load it up with action. We need more action, more special effects, more punching.'

"And you don't have a writer sitting there that says, 'I think the script is too overloaded with action. I think that you need three more dramatic scenes in the script. That really makes the people fall behind you and really root for you, so when you go through these dramas, they're with you.'"

The action writer and the drama writer might clash. Tempers would flare. But there would be nothing wrong with that. The diversity around the table, even the tension, improves the final product.

When Schwarzenegger became governor of California, he took a similar approach to running the nation's largest state. Unlike perhaps any other chief executive in America, he relied on a staff and a group of outside advisers from across the ideological and partisan spectrum.

"Why wouldn't I do the same thing in politics?" he asks. "I come from that background, where you debate with people that agree and disagree, and you want to find the right answer rather than just having one type of people, let's say Republicans, around, just saying one thing, and you never get to know the other side."

Schwarzenegger has certainly grown to know the other side. His first chief of staff was a Republican who had served as a top aide to his political mentor, former governor Pete Wilson. But after two years, Schwarzenegger replaced her with a Democrat. His wife, Maria Shriver, also has a Democrat as her top aide (though for a time she had a Republican). Their longtime friend, Bonnie Reiss, also a Democrat, was a key adviser throughout Schwarzenegger's first term. But Republicans also fill important jobs. The cabinet secretary, who rides herd over the political appointees who actually run the government, is a conservative Republican. And Schwarzenegger's legislative secretaries and finance directors have all been Republicans.

Having not come of age in a partisan political environment, or cut his teeth working his way up the political ladder, Schwarzenegger does not view the world through the kind of partisan lens that is typical among American political leaders. He sees himself as a Republican. But when he looks for advice and advisers, he generally doesn't care what a person's party designation might be. He is most comfortable around people with bold ideas and the ability to express them.

It is a style that benefits Schwarzenegger in a number of ways. Most obviously, it gives him a breadth of advice and points of view that he would never get from a more ideological harmonious set of advisers. He has people around him who challenge his—and each other's—assumptions and raise questions he wouldn't have considered. At a time when President George W. Bush has been criticized for relying on too narrow a cast of advisers, Schwarzenegger stands in stark contrast. When Schwarzenegger makes a major decision, there is little chance that he will be surprised by the public reaction from one side or another. Usually he has already heard it, in the privacy of his own office.

The public got its first look at Schwarzenegger's management style during the 2003 campaign, when he called on billionaire investor Warren Buffett, among others, to advise him on economic policy. Buffett was soon quoted in the *Wall Street Journal* saying that California's property tax system was unfair and outdated, and suggesting that the candidate consider raising taxes if he became governor. Schwarzenegger had no intention of doing any such thing, so he distanced himself from Buffett's advice. Later, when the two appeared together after a meeting of Schwarzenegger's economic advisers, the candidate joked that if the aging Buffett ever brought up the issue again, he'd tell the adviser to drop and give him 500 push-ups.

Schwarzenegger's habit of soliciting advice from diverse sources would hardly be remarkable outside of politics. People do it all the time. But it is less common in our rigidly partisan political system. So when a prominent adviser to a politician, whether paid or unpaid, says something controversial, or openly discusses a potential policy position, it is widely assumed that the statement reflects the thinking of the politician as well. That is not necessarily the case with Schwarzenegger. He enjoys the give and take. But he sees nothing wrong with sparking a conversation and then rejecting the advice that comes out of it.

The Buffett comments got international play, but less attention was focused on another important Schwarzenegger adviser who was more circumspect: George Shultz. The former treasury secretary and secretary of state, a Hoover Institution fellow at Stanford who has argued for cutting taxes and legalizing drugs, quietly presented Schwarzenegger with a plan for restructuring the state's debt that later became the basis for Schwarzenegger's first major policy move as governor.[2] Shultz and Buffett could not be more different. And they were just two soldiers in an army of advisers shut-tling through the candidate's Santa Monica offices.

Being new to organized politics when he first ran for governor, Schwarzenegger had to quickly ramp up a policy shop and flesh out positions on a wide range of issues. Heading a group of advisers who managed that task for him was Joe Rodota, another former Wilson aide. Two years earlier, when Schwarzenegger had briefly contemplated running for governor, Rodota prepared a document he called "Schwarzenegger A to Z" in which he combed through everything Schwarzenegger ever said on the public record that was in any way connected to politics or public policy. This time, Rodota started with that record and then asked Schwarzenegger a battery of questions on all the major public policy issues, trying to elicit his views on any subject that might come up during the campaign.

Where Schwarzenegger's views were well formed, Rodota and other campaign advisers set to work translating the candidate's be-liefs into policy positions and proposals. When Schwarzenegger wasn't sure how he felt about a subject, the staff invited policy ex-perts from across the country to come to Santa Monica to discuss the topics with the candidate in lengthy briefings. These sessions, which took place every other day or so for about a month, quickly became known as "Schwarzenegger University."

The discussions were tightly focused and moved along quickly, more like a corporate executive meeting than a political brain-storming session. One or more of the experts would make a pre-sentation, and then Schwarzenegger would probe with questions.

Although some of the experts brought PowerPoint presenta-tions, there was not a blizzard of paper. The candidate preferred conversation. "He is an auditory learner," Rodota said.[3] If one of the experts strayed into a digression, Schwarzenegger would glance at Rodota and raise an eyebrow, and the aide would interrupt the speaker. "We're in the weeds," Rodota would say, urging the person to get back on point. With the campaign moving at warp speed, there was not a lot of time to waste.

After presentations from 20 or 25 people and background work by dozens more who never met with the candidate, the staff used the information gleaned from the meetings and Schwarzenegger's conclusions from what he'd heard to develop policy proposals on a broad range of topics. Those briefings were then compiled into binders that another policy aide, Paul Miner, carried with him as he traveled with Schwarzenegger for weeks, going over the points with him in his plane, his car, wherever they might be. Although conventional wisdom was that the Schwarzenegger campaign was devoid of substance, the truth was that, at least as measured by policy white papers, it had more substance than the campaign of any other major candidate in the race. He had detailed proposals on workers' compensation, education, the environment, energy, and political reform—every important issue of the day except, notably, the state's massive budget problem, on which Schwarzenegger refused to be pinned down.

After the election, Schwarzenegger chose Republican Patricia Clarey as his chief of staff and put Republicans in most of the key jobs in his inner circle. But he kept his friend Reiss close by as senior adviser. He named Terry Tamminen, a political independent and an environmental activist who had helped him shape his campaign proposals, as head of California's Environmental Protection Agency. His legal counsel was Peter Siggins, who, as a career lawyer in the California Department of Justice, had served in high positions for a very conservative Republican attorney general, Dan Lungren, and a very liberal Democrat, Bill Lockyer. Siggins later served briefly as Schwarzenegger's chief of staff before the governor appointed him to an appellate court judgeship. One of his more telling choices was his adviser on economic policy. For that job he picked David Crane, a friend and a fellow millionaire—and a Democrat who was an unrelenting advocate of free enterprise and free markets.

When making important decisions, Schwarzenegger liked to convene contentious discussions on policy issues among advisers who disagreed. They gathered in the Ronald Reagan Cabinet room in his Capitol office suite or at the governor's residence in the Hyatt Hotel across the street.

"He's spent a lot of years with the Kennedys, and they have a tendency to debate things hotly around the dining room table," Tamminen said.[4] "He's quite used to that and enjoys that. Let's dig into the issue and find out why some people believe differently from others."

Tamminen, who helped steer Schwarzenegger toward bold proposals on greenhouse gases, hydrogen power, solar energy, and ocean protection, said people in the governor's inner circle felt free to express their own views while also sharing a responsibility to help Schwarzenegger advance the agenda he had laid out for the state. Although Tamminen was at the center of some of the staff's most contentious conflicts, he said he always felt he was trying to do what Schwarzenegger wanted, not simply promoting his own personal policy agenda.

"All of us, when we signed on, signed on because we believed in the guy, and we believed he was somebody who transcended typical party labels," he said. "Sometimes he does things that some of us think are to the right. Sometimes he does things that some of us think are to the left. But at the end of the day, it's what he believed in, and what we signed on for, and who he is."[5]

Schwarzenegger also took a bipartisan approach to dealing with the Legislature during his first year in office. Although he had weekly meetings with the Republican leadership, he engaged in frequent banter with the Democrats, who controlled both houses of the Legislature with wide majorities. This is something that is simply not done in Washington, D.C., where the ideological differences and the traditions of the institutions do not allow for such intimate, cross-party contact. It was not exactly normal in Sacramento, either, before Schwarzenegger arrived. But he eagerly gathered lawmakers in his office in small groups to schmooze and pick their brains about the state's priorities. Often, they would smoke cigars in the tent he installed on the open-air patio outside his office suite. Many Democrats said they had more face time with Schwarzenegger in his first five months in office than they had had with former Governor Davis, a fellow Democrat, in five years.

Schwarzenegger built his most famous bipartisan legislative alliance with John Burton, the foul-mouthed, irascible leader of the state senate from San Francisco. Burton was a liberal's liberal who had been in and out of the Legislature and Congress since 1964, the brother of Phil Burton, a legendary powerhouse in Congress in the 1960s and 1970s. A recovered cocaine addict who was intimidated by no one, Burton boycotted Schwarzenegger's inauguration, sending a signal to the newly elected chief executive that he, unlike many others in the Capitol, was not awed by the actor's stardom.

"I think we can have a good working relationship," Burton said early in Schwarzenegger's first term. "But it depends on what the hell he wants to do and who he wants to pay for it. If he wants to balance the budget on the backs of the poor, I don't think so. Not as long as I'm here."[6]

But Schwarzenegger wasn't cowed by Burton, either. He soon turned on the charm. He unleashed Maria Shriver and her mother, Eunice, to soften Burton up by sharing stories of the old days and the Kennedy dynasty. He sent the senator flowers on his birthday, and gave him a boxed set of Alfred Hitchcock films on disc. He broke protocol for a governor by visiting the legislative chambers and by going to see the leaders in their offices, a seemingly small gesture but one that suggested Schwarzenegger did not view himself as the center of the political universe. The governor even joked at one public event that he and Burton were growing so fond of each other that San Francisco Mayor Gavin Newsom might issue them a marriage certificate.

Burton responded. For all his toughness as a legislator, he admitted he was impressed by the little things, including Schwarzenegger's willingness to pay a courtesy call to his office.

"I don't remember the last time a governor would come up to the second floor to talk to the leader of another party," he said.

Early on, Burton ordered Wiener schnitzel from a local restaurant for himself and the governor while they were working late. Later, realizing that he shared a love of espresso with the chief executive, Burton began making trips downstairs with a stainless steel carafe of steamed milk he whipped up for the governor's coffee. Burton would simply wave himself through security into Schwarzenegger's first floor suite of offices. He was there so often that some of the governor's aides began looking over their shoulders before saying anything sensitive involving the Senate, for fear that Burton might be standing there. And the frequent contact helped smooth the way for some of the early deals that the new governor cut with the Legislature.

Schwarzenegger, Burton said, "starts out at one place, and we start out at another place, and he just keeps driving until we get a deal."[7]

The final link in Schwarzenegger's feedback chain was his extensive network of friends and occasional advisers from all over. His wife played a key role—as a sounding board, an unofficial personnel chief, and a watchdog to ensure that everyone in his inner circle was working for the governor's interests and not their own. He consulted occasionally with former governor Wilson, and with Robert Hertzberg, a former Democratic speaker of the State Assembly. He chatted from time to time with Bill Clinton.

Another informal adviser was Leon Panetta, a former congressman who was Clinton's chief of staff in the White House. Panetta said he was impressed by Schwarzenegger's bipartisan style. "It really is kind of a philosophy of, 'What is the best way to get something done?'" Panetta said. "He looks at it more like a businessman would look at decisions. My sense is that's the way he approaches the job."[8]

Schwarzenegger's open-ended information gathering has its strengths, but it also has caused problems. Despite rosy public descriptions of their harmonious working relationship, aides competed for his ear in the hope that he would side with the last person who spoke to him before he made a decision. On some issues, factions developed as aides jockeyed to influence him. Clarey, his first chief of staff, tried to control who went in and out of his office, or at least keep track, but she had little influence over the people with whom he talked in private, at home, or on his cell phone. His staff, over time, grew divided between his old friends, known as "the posse," and his new advisers, several of whom had worked for former governor Wilson.

When things were going well for Schwarzenegger, he wasn't concerned about the tensions.

"I am very good in delegating and in not ever having to worry," he said. "That's not my style, or my way, that I hire someone and then I'm checking out all the time if they're doing things right. I hire someone because I have done enough research that I say this is a great person to have on my team. And then it's over. Then you have the trust. And then sometimes you run into problems that in the end you say, 'Why did I go with that person?' Yes, that happens."[9]

He acknowledged that, after two years in office, he realized he needed to make changes. His operation simply wasn't clicking.

"This is why I am now with the current staff," he said in 2007. "Because you have to weed out. I mean, in the beginning it was difficult. Maybe I did not know sometimes exactly which direction to go in some of the things. So it's hard to blame anyone. It's just that the first year is the first—the beginning is always rough. But then I knew this is the kind of people that I really wanted to have around."

When Schwarzenegger hired Democrat Susan Kennedy to be his new chief of staff in December 2005, the move drew national attention. Kennedy was not just any Democrat, but a former spokeswoman for the California Democratic Party, onetime director of the California Abortion Rights Action League, and even, once, a senior aide to former governor Davis, whom Schwarzenegger had banished in the 2003 recall election. Kennedy was also a lesbian in an open relationship with a woman with whom she had exchanged vows in a marriage ceremony in Maui. She admitted that she had never voted for a Republican in her life—though she did say that she had voted for all four of the ballot initiatives Schwarzenegger had endorsed in a special election, and she intended to vote for him when he ran for reelection.

Republican activists reacted to the hiring with horror. They feared it was a sign that Schwarzenegger had gone over to the other side. Democrats mocked him, suggesting that he was hopelessly confused about what he believed and where he hoped to lead the state. Both turned out to be wrong.

Schwarzenegger hired Kennedy to bring order to the cacophony of voices that surrounded him, and to help him demonstrate an ability to govern that would be crucial to his hopes of a comeback victory in his reelection campaign. Kennedy had been appointed to the state's Public Utilities Commission by Davis, and she and Schwarzenegger first came into contact in discussions about electricity regulation and later about the telecommunications industry. As they grew more comfortable with one another, the two began to discuss the state of Schwarzenegger's operation, and his desire to bring more structure to it. Kennedy offered her ideas on the subject, and, when the governor decided he needed a new chief of staff, he turned to her.

Kennedy saw her job not as moving Schwarzenegger in one direction or another but in giving him as much information as he needed to make a decision and then doing whatever it took to implement the decisions he made.

"He is like an incredibly powerful engine, and it's my job to build a frame that allows him to run at his maximum potential," she said.[10]

He still got advice from all over the ideological spectrum. But that advice tended to come in a more organized, structured way. Over the course of a year, Kennedy put people she could trust—Republicans as well as Democrats—into key positions. Since those people were hired by her, and not directly by Schwarzenegger as was the case with his first staff, they were loyal to her and did not try to go around her to get to the governor. The result, although weighted more to the left than was his first senior staff, was still diverse. But it was a far more cohesive and controlled operation.

No one else in America was doing anything similar to what Schwarzenegger was doing in California. In a hyperpartisan political environment, in which the parties seemed to be moving farther apart by the day, Schwarzenegger was not simply trying to split the difference. He was beginning to blur many of the traditional ideological distinctions and replace them with something new, something that was not so much a compromise between two poles as a unique, organic blend all his own.

That approach was creative, but it did not always work as planned. The biggest problem Schwarzenegger faced as governor would prove all but immune to the charms of his bipartisan style.

PART II

THE GOVERNATOR

Once Schwarzenegger took office and assembled his staff, it was time to govern, and he soon found the job he was elected to do far more difficult than the campaign it took to win the election. The culture into which he stepped as a political novice seemed to dictate one of two approaches. He could either accommodate everyone with lowest-common-denominator solutions that did little, or attack his opponents with a high-decibel, confrontational campaign. He tried both approaches, sometimes simultaneously. Although each method succeeded to a degree, neither worked in the long run. And so he learned on the job, adjusted, and evolved. It was a wild ride. Here is that story.

FOUR

Fusion

In his first hours as a candidate for governor, in his first press conference as a politician, outside the Burbank studios of Jay Leno's *Tonight Show*, Schwarzenegger captured his governing philosophy in a few sentences lost in the crush of international media swarming the celebrity candidate.

"The most important thing is that we bring business back to California," Schwarzenegger said. "There are more businesses leaving California now than ever before. When businesses come back, revenue comes back. When revenue comes back, we can afford all kinds of different programs that are very important. We want to make sure that the children are not left without any books. We want to make sure that our children have the books, that they have their place in the classroom. We want to make sure that they have after-school programs. We want to make sure the mothers have affordable day care. We want to make sure the older folks have their care that they need."[1]

Schwarzenegger's claim that businesses were fleeing California in droves was an exaggeration that he repeated often but never backed up with solid evidence. There was no dispute, however, that California's economy was flat. Or that the state government was in the midst of a fiscal crisis that threatened its ability to provide health, education, and welfare services to those who needed them most.

What made Schwarzenegger's statement unique was its fusion of right and left.[2] He combined a strong support for business with a bold and unequivocal endorsement of government programs and services—literally from cradle to grave. Republicans often promote business-friendly policies for their own sake, out of an ideological belief in individual freedom or a sense that a stronger business climate will mean more jobs and better opportunity for all. Democrats often speak of the need for higher government revenues to provide the kind of services that they and their constituents value. But here was a politician doing both. Schwarzenegger was proclaiming the need to promote economic growth in order to generate more revenues for government programs. It was a blending of priorities and approaches that defined him as a politician. Although it didn't get much notice in the press at the time, and although it was certainly overshadowed by the circus atmosphere of the recall election and the celebrity focus of Schwarzenegger's own campaign, this was the best statement of a Schwarzenegger core for which so many analysts would be searching for years to come. It was also the source of many of the internal conflicts with which he would wrestle as governor.

He was, in this way, a mirror of the state he hoped to lead. Poll after poll has shown that Californians, like most Americans, don't want to pay higher taxes. But neither do they want to cut spending on education, health care, transportation, or public assistance for the poor. They want it all. They just don't want to pay more for it. That was Schwarzenegger's essential approach as well.

Out of personal conviction and political necessity, he stood firmly against new taxes throughout his first campaign and his first term in office. This is what marked him as a conservative, what gave Republicans something with which to identify in a candidate who supported abortion rights, gay rights, and government intervention to protect the environment.

Schwarzenegger's opposition to higher taxes dated back to his days as an informal student of the writings of Milton Friedman, the free-market economist whom Schwarzenegger met and befriended. Even before he ran for office, Schwarzenegger was so strongly identified with the anti-tax movement that he was the honored speaker at a 25th anniversary gala for Proposition 13, the fabled California ballot measure that capped property taxes in 1978 and started an anti-tax wave that eventually helped Ronald Reagan win the White House. As a candidate, Schwarzenegger put his anti-tax position front and center in his first extended meeting with the political press, after a session with his economic advisers at a hotel near Los Angeles International Airport on August 20, 2003. In retrospect, Schwarzenegger probably could have won the election had he simply said that taxes would be a last resort in any plan he would propose to balance the state budget. But he went further than that, saying flatly that he would not raise taxes as part of any fiscal plan. Californians, he said, were already taxed enough.

"From the time they get up in the morning and flush the toilet, they're taxed," he said. "When they go and get coffee, they're taxed. They get into their car, they're taxed. They go to the gas station, they're taxed. They go for lunch, they're taxed. This goes on all day long. Tax, tax, tax, tax, tax. Even when they go to bed, you can go to bed in fear that you are going to be taxed while you're sleeping, that there is a sleeping tax."[3]

Polling data at the time did not suggest that Californians felt overwhelmed by their tax burden, which hovered around the top 10 among the states nationally but was not at the very top. There was some anger, however, especially among Republicans, about one tax in particular. California's vehicle license fee, or "car tax," had for decades been set at 2 percent of the vehicle's value, or about $600 a year for a car worth $30,000. But Pete Wilson, as governor in the late 1990s during a time of huge budget surpluses, had set in motion a series of reductions that brought the levy to a third of its former level. As part of a compromise with the Democrats in the Legislature, those tax cuts were accompanied by an unusual provision that allowed the rate to go back up again if the state hit tough fiscal times. Governor Gray Davis, facing a big shortfall in the summer of 2003, had triggered that provision, tripling the tax and returning it to its former level. Conservatives were outraged by the tax being raised and the way Davis did it, without a vote of the Legislature. They rallied an electorate that, given California's affinity for the automobile, didn't need much encouragement. Now Schwarzenegger promised to undo Davis's action and lower the car tax yet again. At a rally in the Orange County town of Costa Mesa, his campaign dropped a 3,600-pound wrecking ball on an Oldsmobile to signal what he intended to do to the car tax.

"In the movies, if I played a character and I didn't like something, you know what I did? I destroyed it!" he declared as the ball hung over the car. "I wiped it out!" With that, the ball dropped, and the car was flattened. The crowd roared.[4]

With campaign events like that, there was no going back once Schwarzenegger won the election. In the days following the vote, he came under mounting pressure from Democrats, political activists, interest groups, and newspaper editorial boards to renounce his pledge and leave the car tax where it was. His task of balancing the budget certainly would have been much easier had he taken this counsel. The car tax produced nearly $4 billion a year, and his promise meant that the state's budget shortfall would rise from about $10 billion to $14 billion in his first year—on a budget of about $80 billion. But the calls for Schwarzenegger to abandon his pledge, while perhaps realistic as bottom-line analyses of the budget, were cynical in the extreme. Schwarzenegger had just spent the entire campaign promising to roll back the tax. If the brand new governor had backed off at that point, any credibility he enjoyed as a citizen-politician would have vanished, and the power that came from his outsider, celebrity status would have disappeared. He would have been just like any other pol, breaking his promises as soon as he took office. Republicans would have deserted him, and many independents and Democrats, already skeptical, would have concluded from Day One that he could not be taken seriously. So he kept the promise, and rolled back the tax with an executive order. He signed it, with great fanfare, a few minutes after taking the oath of office on November 17.

But almost as soon as he had nailed down his right flank with that order, Schwarzenegger began tacking left. Having cut one tax and promised not to raise any others, he was staring at a massive deficit, and the spending cuts necessary to balance the budget in one year would have been unthinkable, even for most Republicans. An audit he had promised during the campaign, and which he had implied would point the way to balancing the budget, was never going to bear that kind of fruit. It was downgraded to a quick, broad study of the state's financial picture that offered no solutions to the intractable problem he had inherited.

Instead, Schwarzenegger and his advisers proposed a multiyear plan built around a bond measure that would restructure the state's deficit and borrow some more to help ease the way back to a balanced budget. It was like refinancing your home to get a better interest rate, consolidating your debts, and then taking some cash out to buy a new car. They would slow the growth in spending over time, the governor's finance team said, and hope that an economic recovery would lift revenues and bring spending and tax receipts back into balance.

Schwarzenegger took a lot of heat from both the right and the left for his deficit bond measure, which at the time was the largest single borrowing by any state government in American history. But this restructuring of the debt was not only politically smart; it might have been a legal necessity. Davis, before leaving office, had crafted a budget that relied on a $10 billion deficit bond that he intended for the state to sell without a vote of the people. The California constitution, however, prohibited borrowing more than

$300,000 without such a public vote. By the time Schwarzenegger took office, taxpayer groups had already sued the state to try to stop the borrowing. Had that lawsuit prevailed, he would have been left with a massive hole in the budget, a cash-flow crisis of unprecedented proportions, and, perhaps, an insolvent government unable to pay its bills and at the mercy of its Wall Street creditors.

The real problem with Schwarzenegger's plan was not the bond itself, but the lack of any discipline to rein in spending along with it. It might have made sense to borrow more if that borrowing were accompanied by a detailed workout plan, a road map to recovery that the entire state could see, understand, and buy into. Had he used his support for more borrowing as a hammer to get legislators to commit to hold spending growth to, say, 5 percent a year for three years, he could have fixed the problem. But this he failed to do.

Instead, he at first proposed a permanent, strict new limit on state spending that the Democrats were never going to accept. Then, when the Democrats balked, he quickly capitulated. He agreed to substitute a measure that he said would require a balanced budget and a larger rainy day fund. But he let the Democrats write it, and they inserted so many loopholes that the final product required neither a balanced budget nor a true reserve. Schwarzenegger accepted the deal because he was desperate to show progress on the budget deficit in the first real test of his ability to work with the Legislature. A handful of Republican lawmakers, not willing to let their governor fail in his first major enterprise, held their noses and voted for the measures. And to the ballot they went.

The election that followed, in March 2004, was the first vivid display of the kind of over-the-top bipartisanship that Schwarzenegger would later make his trademark. The deficit bonds started out far behind in the polls, but Schwarzenegger campaigned for them relentlessly. Much of the time he did so with the Democratic state controller, former eBay executive Steve Westly, at his side. At more than one event, Schwarzenegger cut a giant fake credit card in two to emphasize his position that the balanced budget amendment would end deficit spending forever in California. Both the California Democratic Party and the state Republican Party endorsed the measures, as did just about every interest group with a stake in state government. Even U.S. Senator Dianne Feinstein, the state's most popular politician, campaigned with the governor. The only vocal opposition came from a conservative Republican state senator—Tom McClintock—who favored budget cuts instead, and the state's treasurer, Democrat Phil Angelides, who wanted the state to raise taxes rather than borrow to cover its deficit. But there was no serious, organized campaign waged against the measures, and in the end, the bonds passed with a vote of 63 percent to 37 percent. The balanced budget amendment did even better, winning by a margin of 71 percent to 29 percent. The results were an early indication of Schwarzenegger's cross-partisan appeal. Republicans backed his borrowing by a margin of 76 percent to 24 percent, a result that no Democrat ever could have dreamed of getting. Yet 58 percent of Democrats and 59 percent of independents also voted for the deficit bond.[5]

"We have removed the financial sword that was hanging over California's head," Schwarzenegger said in a victory speech at a Santa Monica hotel. "We can now refinance the inherited debt and we can move forward. We have sent a strong signal to Wall Street to let them know that we are putting our problems behind us."[6]

But borrowing more money was the easy part. For all his bold talk, Schwarzenegger never really had the stomach to make the kind of cuts that would have been necessary to balance the budget in the absence of a tax hike. He fed the right wing with his rhetoric from time to time, but his actions rarely lived up to his words. He promised to "blow up the boxes" on the state organization chart with a radical restructuring of government, but after a plan he commissioned drew protests from its targets and their allies, he dropped it. He called Democrats "spending addicts" and promised to "starve the monster" of state government, echoing a phrase made famous by Grover Norquist, a prominent Washington-based movement conservative. But when it came time to actually write and sign a budget, Schwarzenegger didn't have the nerve to follow through.

As his first finance director, Schwarzenegger had recruited Donna Arduin, a soft-spoken but hard-nosed conservative who was working for Governor Jeb Bush in Florida. As her first step in attacking the problem, Arduin proposed to slash projected spending on health and welfare programs. She wanted to cut welfare grants for poor single mothers; suspend a cost-of-living increase in stipends to the aged, blind, and disabled; and kill an open-ended entitlement for poor kids' health insurance—directly contradicting a Schwarzenegger campaign promise to expand that program to all children who needed it. Arduin thought Schwarzenegger was serious about cutting spending, and as a newcomer to California and to Schwarzenegger's inner circle, she was politically tone deaf. The new governor, surprisingly, wasn't much better. And so his first budget proposal even called for the repeal of a pioneering California law that guaranteed access to care for the developmentally disabled—the same group of people who had become the life's work of the governor's mother-in-law, Eunice Kennedy Shriver.

Schwarzenegger quickly dropped that idea. It was wrong, he said, and he conceded that he had proposed it in haste, without realizing what he was doing. As the protests mounted and the state's revenue picture improved marginally, the new governor abandoned many of Arduin's other suggestions as well, dropping some of the spending cuts unilaterally and others in negotiations with the Legislature. After a call from one of his daughters alerted him to the outcry over a proposal to save the counties $14 million by speeding the euthanizing of cats and dogs in animal shelters, he disowned that idea. A more traditional Sacramento interest, the transportation lobby, persuaded him to back away from a plan to cut dedicated highway funds to pay for general state programs. He made it a loan instead. And the state employee unions made it clear that they were not going to agree to salary cuts or any significant change in their pension benefits. After the governor accepted a face-saving proposal on pensions and appeared at a union executives meeting in Sacramento, he received a standing ovation, hardly the sort of reception you would expect for a man who had promoted himself as a fiscal hardliner.

In the end, Schwarzenegger signed a budget in the summer of 2004 that spent $2.6 billion more than he had proposed in January of that year, and about $6 billion more than the first spending limit he had demanded in the Legislature but then withdrew. That budget did spend less than would have been required by the automatic spending formulas in the budget. But many of the cuts he managed to enact came with a twist. Schwarzenegger negotiated a series of backroom deals with stakeholders in the public schools, the universities, and local government. In each case, supporters of those programs agreed to short-term spending reductions in exchange for the governor's commitment to support more spending down the road. This tactic allowed him to show some progress toward balancing the budget in his first year. It bought him some time. But it also set in place a series of fiscal time bombs that would keep him from balancing the books throughout his first term in office. One of those bombs, a deal he made with the teachers union over public school funding, blew up in his face a year later and plunged his governorship into crisis.

Schwarzenegger's failure to deal with the long-term, structural problem in the budget—the fact that spending was programmed by law to grow faster than tax revenues—allowed state spending to rise from $78 billion when he took office to $102 billion as he ran for reelection three years later, an increase of more than 30 percent. Some of that was misleading, due to the state's unique system of accounting. The cut in the car tax, for instance, showed up in the books as an increase in state spending, because the tax was a local revenue source and the state was obliged to reimburse cities and counties for the money they lost when the tax rate was reduced. Also, Governor Davis's final budget had shifted more than $1 billion in health spending from the end of one year to the beginning of the next, inflating that number in Schwarzenegger's first year in office and making it look as if the new governor were increasing spending on health care for the poor.

But most of the spending growth on his watch was very real. By the time he was reelected in November 2006, the state was spending more per capita and more as a percentage of the economy than it ever had before.[7] Per-pupil spending in the schools grew by 17 percent on his watch. Services for mentally disabled people grew by 32 percent, as did spending on care for elderly and disabled people confined to their homes. Health care grew by 15 percent. Spending on the state's troubled prison system exploded by 71 percent.[8]

Republican lawmakers grumbled about these numbers, but enough of them voted for the budget each year to provide the two-thirds majorities needed for approval. Schwarzenegger continued to complain that the state's constitution and its laws required too many automatic spending increases, and, in 2005, he asked the voters for enhanced authority to cut spending on his own. But the voters rejected his proposal. He eased off in 2006, his reelection year, but in 2007, Schwarzenegger proposed more cuts. He asked the Legislature to end welfare grants to families headed by an able-bodied adult who refused to work or had been on aid for five years. He tried to suspend cost-of-living raises to welfare recipients and the aged, blind, and disabled. And he suggested setting aside a formula that directed a portion of the sales tax to local transit, proposing to use more than $1 billion for other purposes. He also offered a couple of short-term budget gimmicks to stave off more deficits, at least temporarily. He proposed to sell a quasi-public business that serviced student loans, and he asked lawmakers to consider leasing the state lottery to a private investor who would pay, potentially, tens of billions of dollars up front. "We got creative," he told reporters when asked to explain his budget strategy.[9]

Schwarzenegger, over time, discovered what most Republicans in government eventually learn: Republican voters actually like most government spending, even if they think they oppose it in the abstract. Republicans have children in the public schools, they drive on state highways, and they have family members who are mentally ill or developmentally disabled. Any politician who tries to cut those programs will run afoul of voters from across the ideological spectrum. Democrats will see them as heartless and cold. And Republicans will not exactly rush to their aid. There simply is not much of a viable voting constituency for cutting spending when people can feel and understand what is being cut.

Like the voters, Schwarzenegger did not really want to shrink the size of government, no matter what he might have said in the heat of the battle. He simply wanted the books to balance. And with state revenues buoyed by another bull market on Wall Street and the reemergence of the state's high-tech economy, Schwarzenegger was able to make some progress toward balancing the budget without having to raise taxes in his first three years in office. But in the budget he signed in 2006, spending still exceeded revenues by more than $6 billion, with the gap closed by money from an unexpected surge in tax receipts the year before. A year later, he was able to erase that gap on paper, signing a budget that matched revenues and spending for one year. But projections showed that the balance would be short lived. Once again, by 2008, spending was expected to outstrip tax revenues by $5 billion. That was a precarious situation for the state. Years into an economic recovery, the government should not have been spending more than it was taking in. If another recession hit and tax revenues dropped again, the big deficits were sure to grow, perhaps to unmanageable proportions. Eventually, Schwarzenegger would probably be forced to try to raise taxes. Yet by putting off that day for as long as possible, Schwarzenegger was able to keep his Republican base satisfied. And by moderating his push to cut spending, he was able to calm the Democrats who had turned against him earlier in his tenure.

His goal of bringing the state's books back into the black—the defining issue in his first campaign for the governor's office—would continue to depend on little more than a gamble, a hope that the economy would perform better than his own experts expected. It might have been a good formula for political success. But as fiscal policy, it would never get the job done.

FIVE

Taking Care of Business

Even as Schwarzenegger shied away from the tough decisions needed to balance the budget, he stuck, for the most part, to his alliance with the business community. As a business owner himself, he identified with the entrepreneur and the mogul alike; having mostly shed his European roots, he believed strongly in the power of individuals. He was willing, sometimes eager, to use government to create opportunity for all. But he still thought it was each person's responsibility to take advantage of that opportunity, and he viewed investors and business owners as the risk-takers who made the good life possible for everyone else. Even when he advocated policies that the business community opposed, he almost never used corporations as political punching bags. Rather, he maintained his pro-business rhetoric and persuaded himself that those policies were either inconsequential to employers or would actually help businesses in the long run, whether they realized it or not. But for most of his first term, on most of the issues they cared about, he stood by his business supporters as a loyal ally and partner.

In this, as in so many other things, Schwarzenegger sought a middle ground that eluded most of his fellow politicians in Sacramento and Washington, D.C. He built a reputation as a friend to business and as a fan of capitalism, growth, dynamism, and competition. This was the one thing that most set him apart from the Democrats in the Legislature with whom he otherwise worked so

closely. But he also parted ways with the Republicans by being willing to consider new regulations on business if he could be convinced that they were justified. This straddle often left him isolated
on economic issues within the walls of the Capitol. But it appealed
to the broad middle of the electorate, people who judge the value
of public policy more on common sense than ideological litmus
tests.

Still, his warm relationship with the business community—and
corporate America's generous financial support for his campaigns—
left Schwarzenegger vulnerable to the charge that he was captive
to big business. He had famously said in his coming-out on the
Leno show that he did not "need" anybody's money because he
was a wealthy man himself. That statement left the distinct impression that he was promising not to take special interest dollars.
But he never had any intention of abstaining from private contributions. At home in Brentwood that night after his announcement,
he was already on the telephone to potential donors asking for
their help.

One of his first calls was to Orange County, the wealthy Republican hotbed where members of the New Majority, a group of moderate Republican business executives, were gathered that night at
the exclusive Pacific Club in Newport Beach.[1] The group was meeting with Gerald Parsky, President Bush's closest adviser in California and long an advocate for transforming the California Republican Party into a more moderate, pro-business organization rather
than one focused on social conservative causes. A speaker phone
was brought into the room so that Schwarzenegger could address
them all at once.

"He wanted us to know he was running for governor," Lawrence
Higby, a health-care executive and chairman of the group, said
later. "He said it had been a very difficult decision, that he and his
wife had thought a lot about it and decided to do it. He was totally
committed to running an administration that would bring back not

only dignity but fiscal responsibility to the state of California and return it to the golden state that it is."

Higby's group had worked with Schwarzenegger before, as major supporters of a ballot measure the actor had sponsored in 2002 to pour more money into after-school programs. They soon endorsed him for governor, and the members became some of his most loyal donors. Other business leaders followed their example. Over the next three years he would raise more than $100 million for his own campaigns and for the ballot measures he supported, setting him on course to be the most prolific fundraiser in California history.[2]

According to one account, Schwarzenegger raised nearly $18 million from banks and financial firms, $17 million from real estate and construction companies, and $12 million from the entertainment industry in his first three years as a candidate and governor.[3] Three donors each gave him or his causes more than $2 million: Spanish-language television tycoon Jerry Perenchio; developer and San Diego Chargers owner Alex Spanos; and William Robinson, founder of the DHL courier service. The governor's million-dollar club included Ameriquest Capital Corp.; Henry Nicholas, chairman of N3 Holdings LLC; and B. Wayne Hughes, chairman of Public Storage Inc.

Pressed to square his voracious appetite for campaign cash with his vow to sweep the "special interests" from the Capitol, Schwarzenegger insisted that the loyalty was a one-way street. His many corporate donors, he said, were supporting him because they believed in his cause, but he said he had little knowledge of specific favors they sought—and no intention of granting any.

"I never said I would not accept money, that special interests are no good and would not be part of the mix," he said. "I said we have to stop the money from going in and the favors from going out. . . . I cannot be bought by anyone, and anyone who gives me money buys into that philosophy."[4]

On one important issue early in his term, Schwarzenegger found a topic that allowed him to argue for both the business owner and the employee: the state's troubled system for compensating workers who were injured on the job. This was a problem he had first spotlighted during the 2003 campaign, when, in meetings with business owners large and small, he got an earful about the rising costs of the program. California employers paid the highest rates in the nation for the insurance, yet workers who were injured got some of the lowest benefits. And the program was failing in other ways: California workers injured on the job took longer to get back to work, either because the program failed to cure and retrain them or because the incentives were aligned toward keeping them idle and at home. In any case, Schwarzenegger adopted the issue as his own and, remarkably, managed to make "workers' compensation" something of a household phrase in California.

Emboldened by his ballot victories on the deficit bond and the balanced budget amendment in early 2004, Schwarzenegger declared that fixing workers' compensation would be his next big goal. He set a deadline for the Legislature to act and warned that he would go to the voters if lawmakers failed to pass a bill. Then he began raising money to pay for a campaign to gather signatures for a ballot initiative drafted by his business allies.

"It is extremely important that we get rid of the poison of our economy, which is workers' compensation costs," Schwarzenegger told a cheering crowd at a Sacramento rally to gather signatures for the measure. "We are losing jobs continuously because of the high costs."[5]

Labor activists seethed as Schwarzenegger, in alliance with the owners of the Costco retail chain, used workers at the giant stores as volunteers to collect signatures for an initiative that the unions said would hurt working people. But his focus on the issue seemed to sink in. One independent poll of heavily Democratic Los Angeles County found that voters did not want to reduce benefit levels for injured workers, but they responded favorably to descriptions of the kind of complex changes Schwarzenegger was proposing as a way to save money for business. Sixty-four percent said they would vote yes on such a measure, while just 28 percent said they were opposed.[6] With numbers like that, and with his own personal popularity rising, Schwarzenegger had the wind at his back and Democrats were unwilling to stand in his way. After several false starts and missed deadlines, they came to the table.

By the time they did, Schwarzenegger had raised $5 million from his base of business donors and collected most of the one million signatures he would need to place the measure on the ballot if he wanted to do so. He and his allies dropped the initiative once a legislative deal was reached. But his successful use of the ballot measure as leverage in the Legislature, and the Democrats' acquiescence, taught him a lesson that would come back to haunt him later.

The final bill was a compromise that fell short of what business interests were seeking but went much further than Democrats would have done on their own. It standardized benefits according to accepted medical guidelines, gave injured workers immediate access to care, and gave employers more incentives to get workers back on the job. It was supposed to increase benefits for the most severely injured workers while cutting them back for those whose ailments were more minor. The compromise won the backing of insurance companies, employers, and doctors. The California Labor Federation, a coalition of unions that typically opposed any cut in benefits, was neutral. Only the lawyers that made their living representing injured workers remained opposed among the major interest groups with a stake in the issue.

Although Schwarzenegger, as a private employer himself, took an interest in many of the details of the deal, the idea of a bipartisan agreement that had broad support from a range of interest groups seemed almost as important to him as the reform itself. The complex agreement on this vexing problem was a symbol of his desire to change the culture in Sacramento, to break through partisan log-jams and get things done.

"When I came to Sacramento in November, the first thing I heard was that it can't be done," the governor said after the Legislature passed the bill. "By working together, we have shown that we are bigger than our problems, that everything is possible. And I have to say it is a big change that is taking place in this building."[7]

That bill and another reform measure the Legislature passed on the eve of the recall election eventually were credited with cutting insurance premiums by more than 50 percent, saving employers more than $10 billion a year. The bill worked so well, in fact, that many Democrats later regretted voting for the Schwarzenegger package and tried to roll back some of its provisions. Especially controversial were regulations that the governor's administration adopted to implement the bill, which critics said reduced benefits for the most severely injured workers—the very people who were supposed to gain from the new law. Schwarzenegger, though, refused to consider rolling back the changes. With so few concrete accomplishments on his record by the time he ran for reelection, he was not going to backpedal on one achievement that was producing tangible benefits, at least to employers.

But not everything he did for business interests proved to be so popular. On at least two occasions, Schwarzenegger stepped into nasty disputes between employers and labor that left him looking like a tool of big corporations. He might have been right on the policy. But in both cases he was arguably abusing the process, and both would end badly for the governor.

Just before Christmas in 2004, Schwarzenegger proposed emergency regulations that would have allowed employees to work five hours, rather than four, before taking a 30-minute lunch break. The new rules also would have repealed a state mandate that required employers to force their workers to take breaks rather than simply alerting them to the fact that they had a right to a 30-minute respite. The idea, Schwarzenegger aides said, was to give part-time workers more flexibility to work through a lunch break if they wished. And surely many part-time employees would prefer to work five hours and then take lunch on their own time than work only four hours because the state mandates that they then be given a break.

But organized labor and its Democratic Party allies in the Legislature didn't see it that way. They accused Schwarzenegger of doing the bidding of big business, and of Wal-Mart in particular. The giant big-box retailer had been a major donor to the Republican Party, contributing $100,000 at the time of the recall election and another $100,000-plus in 2004. At the time the company was in a dispute with its employees over lunch breaks and had been sued in an Alameda County lawsuit alleging that it had denied its workers the time off they were due, a lawsuit Wal-Mart would later lose. One of the changes Schwarzenegger sought was to limit the time that workers would have to sue over alleged violations, from four years after an incident occurred to just one.

"This is quite a Christmas present to employers," one lawyer said about the proposed regulation. Democratic leaders, in a letter to the state agency that was charged with reviewing the rule change, said it would "effectively eviscerate an employee's right to receive a meal period at all."[8]

Eventually, the courts ruled that Schwarzenegger's use of emergency regulations to address the issue was illegal, and the governor dropped the matter, but not before straining his relations with labor leaders and damaging his reputation as a fair-minded leader who would look out for the interests of working people.

Then there were the nurses. Shortly after Schwarzenegger took office, California's hospital industry approached his administration about new rules that were forcing them to increase the number of nurses on duty at any particular time. For years the hospitals had been held to a medical standard, required to provide safe care but leaving it to their own judgment about how many nurses it would take to do so. But Governor Gray Davis had signed legislation requiring hospitals to provide a minimum number of registered nurses in emergency rooms, operating and recovery rooms, intensive care units and acute care wards, and requiring the state's Department of Health Services to decide what those numbers should be. The standards were to be phased in over time, but Schwarzenegger intervened, issuing emergency regulations to suspend the timetable.

Setting nurse-patient ratios through state law was questionable at best as public policy, given the wide range of conditions, the varied experience of different hospitals' nursing staffs, and the rapid introduction of technology into hospital operations. But Schwarzenegger's attempt to overturn the law through the regulatory process was ham-handed, and it infuriated the California Nurses Association. The union considered the staffing rules to be among the union's most important achievements, and the CNA was using the issue as part of a national recruiting effort to expand into other states. The union sued to force Schwarzenegger to back down. More importantly, the nurses began picketing at nearly every one of his public events. After several nurses unfurled a critical banner as Schwarzenegger addressed a women's business conference in Long Beach late in 2004, the governor told his audience that the protestors were "special interests" upset because he had been "kicking their butts" in Sacramento. He later said he did not know that the demonstrators were nurses. But the union embraced his slur and reveled in it. The moment became a rallying cry for the opposition to the ballot measures Schwarzenegger proposed in 2005, and it helped cement in the public's mind an image of Schwarzenegger as a mean-spirited bully whose goal in office was to serve the powerful, not the people. Eventually, he lost in the courts on that issue, too.

Neither defeat, however, shook his alliance with the business community. He continued to stand squarely with the California Chamber of Commerce against what the group liked to call "job killer" bills, by which it meant anything the chamber did not want to see become law. The governor vetoed all 10 such measures that came to his desk in 2004. Among them were bills to regulate the credit practices of car dealers, cap growth in the Los Angeles ports, increase penalties for gender pay equity violations, increase the minimum wage, and regulate overseas outsourcing by private firms. He had a similar record on bills tracked by the California Taxpayers Association.

There were cases—from offshore oil drilling to prescription drugs, global warming, and health insurance—where he went against the wishes of some of his biggest donors. But the impression created by the broad connection between his corporate contributors and his pro-business policies was undeniable. By the end of his first year in office, only 5 percent of California voters thought he had done "a great deal" to fulfill his promise to reduce the power of special interests in Sacramento. However, since voters tended to expect so little in this regard from any of their political leaders, they didn't seem to hold it against him. Yet. His famous promise, and the voters' perception that he had failed to fulfill it, would later become an effective weapon in the hands of his opponents.

But for now, in late 2004, Schwarzenegger's mixture of right and left on economic issues, standing up for business, cutting taxes while still allowing spending to grow at a modest rate, had sent his public approval ratings soaring. In a survey taken in September 2004 by the nonpartisan Field Poll, 65 percent said they approved of the job he was doing, and only 22 percent were not satisfied, making him one of the most popular governors in the history of the state. That gave Schwarzenegger the confidence he needed to roar into 2005 with an expanded agenda, a more confrontational stance, and enough hubris to nearly cost him his job.

SIX

Year of Reform

Schwarzenegger was on a roll when 2005 began. He had restructured the state's debt, sponsored a balanced budget amendment that the voters embraced, and overhauled the workers' compensation system to the delight of his business backers. He negotiated a budget that appeared to trim the state's projected deficit, and he backed the winning side on 11 of the 15 measures on the November ballot. His ballot victories included a serious, long-term reform he brokered to protect city and county finances from raids by the state and a $3 billion bond measure to jump-start the kind of stem-cell research that the Bush Administration in Washington had refused to allow with federal funds.

Here was a Republican governor, a novice at politics, who seemed to be making rapid progress solving the state's long-standing problems while somehow winning praise from the Democrats who had controlled the California Legislature for most of the past half-century. Not surprisingly, the voters loved it. There was even talk of amending the U.S. Constitution to allow Schwarzenegger, an immigrant, to run for president. In less than 14 months in office after a bitter, contentious recall election, he had quickly built a reservoir of good will with the voters and had accumulated a large amount of political capital. He soon started spending it.

Although his first year in office was widely viewed as a success, and although Schwarzenegger himself was busy selling voters on the story of a California comeback, he decided late in 2004 to make an abrupt change in the way he approached the job. Rather than continue to move forward with incremental steps, challenging the Legislature, sometimes making threats, but then backing down and compromising, Schwarzenegger decided to go for broke. Rather than declaring everything rosy—"fantastic" had quickly become his trademark word—Schwarzenegger began talking more bluntly about the state's many lingering problems. In a speech to the Legislature as the year began, he proposed a series of policy changes and government reforms. Then he issued an ultimatum to lawmakers: pass this program, he said, or he would place his measures on the ballot and call a special election to enact them. It was a bold and daring move. But it would fail spectacularly.

At the time, and in much of the instant history written of this disastrous gambit, Schwarzenegger was described as taking a sharp ideological turn to the right. In reality, his tactics changed more than his ideology. He became much more confrontational, at least in public, with members of the Legislature and their leadership. He returned to the easy rhetorical crutches that had marked his first campaign: tired Hollywood references and personal put-downs of his political foes. And always the eager salesman, he overstated the sweep of the measures he was offering, making them sound far more transformative than they really were.

The proposals at the heart of his new agenda were hardly right wing, nor were they revolutionary. His budget reform was mostly a mix of measures that academics and editorial writers had been recommending for years. His proposal to have an independent commission draw the state's political district boundaries borrowed ideas for which good-government types had long argued—and it was opposed by many Republican lawmakers. His education proposals, calling for teacher pay to be based on merit rather than seniority and requiring teachers to work longer before gaining tenured status, amounted to tinkering around the edges. His most

far-reaching idea was to scrap guaranteed pensions for public employees and replace them with individual investment accounts of
the kind increasingly common in the private sector. But even that
proposal did not seem to offend California's left-leaning voters
when they first heard about it. More than 60 percent said they favored it, and some of his other ideas fared almost as well. Fully
two-thirds of voters said they were happy that Schwarzenegger had
called a special session of the Legislature to deal with those issues.

Handled differently, these or other reform ideas might have won
the favor of the voters that year. But any cross-party potential in the
governor's agenda was lost beneath the combative tone Schwarzenegger set from the start. And when the Democrats in the Legislature decided to oppose him rather than negotiate, the state returned
to exactly the kind of partisan warfare and gridlock that Schwarzenegger had promised to end. He lost the trust of the voters, and he
never offered a compelling reason for either his proposals or for the
special election he called to enact them. Every good political campaign needs a story, a narrative with which voters can identify and
connect. In 2005, Schwarzenegger had no such story, only a collection of proposals that didn't seem to fit together. He allowed his opponents to define him and his ideas on their terms, and they effectively used his own cartoonish acts and rhetoric against him.

The beginning of the end of Schwarzenegger's honeymoon probably came on a warm summer day in 2004 at a Southern California
shopping mall where he had gone to campaign for his budget,
which was then stalled in the Legislature. In the days before his visit
to the city of Ontario, east of Los Angeles, the governor had been
deep in private negotiations with the Democratic leaders. But now
he began to attack them in public as tools of liberal interest groups,
and the personal insult he hurled at them, while buried at the end of
a mangled passage, drew national attention.

"If they don't have the guts to come out here in front of you and
say, 'I don't want to represent you, I want to represent those special

interests, the unions, the trial lawyers, and I want them to make the millions of dollars' . . . If they don't have the guts, I call them girlie men," Schwarzenegger said.[1]

That punch line, ironically, was borrowed from a 1980s television skit that mocked Schwarzenegger, who was then just a rising star in Hollywood. But now, as the celebrity governor turned the line against his opponents, he was accused of sexism and homophobia, not to mention hyperpartisanship.

"It's really painful to hear the governor resort to such blatant homophobia," said Senator Sheila Kuehl, a Santa Monica Democrat who was the first openly lesbian member of the California Legislature. "It's an old-fashioned way of talking about gay men as to indicate they're not as strong. So that part is really painful. And I have to say it's really surprising. It's like he can't get his way so he resorts to some kind of name-calling."[2]

Tempers on all sides soon calmed, and Schwarzenegger got his budget. But there were other early signs—even amid a mainly warm and fuzzy first year in office—that partisan conflict would loom in Schwarzenegger's future. His campaign appearances for President George W. Bush—at the Republican national convention in New York and in the crucial state of Ohio on the weekend before the election—left him in a position to claim partial credit (or be blamed) for the narrow reelection of a president who lost California by more than one million votes. His attempt to defeat Democratic legislators in a handful of districts failed across the board, serving only to remind voters that he was still a Republican in a state where Republicans were badly outnumbered. And the Legislature, in an effort to expose his more conservative side, had sent him a number of popular bills that they knew he would veto.

All of this began to undercut the good vibe Schwarzenegger had developed with independent voters and with Democrats who had voted against him in 2003 but who watched him with an open mind as he found his way in the job. Then came his budget bombshell. In

early January 2005, just as he was laying out his package of reforms, the governor released his annual spending proposal. In it he
disclosed that he was going to break a deal he had made with the
education lobby the year before. Back then, in office for only a few
weeks and desperate for ways to bring his first budget into balance,
Schwarzenegger met privately with the leaders of the California
Teachers Association (the state's largest teachers union) and other
members of a coalition of public school stakeholders. The education lobbyists stunned Capitol insiders—and their Democratic
allies—by dropping their traditional opposition to any spending
cuts. They agreed not to oppose a one-year suspension of California's constitutionally mandated minimum level of funding for
the schools. In return, Schwarzenegger agreed to resume financing
the schools one year later at whatever level the constitution's formula dictated. The agreement saved Schwarzenegger $2 billion in
the short term, allowing him to shift that money to other programs.
But in the long run it gave him nothing but grief.

Now, in January 2005, Schwarzenegger finally realized why the
education lobbyists were happy to make that deal. He also learned
that he had not fully grasped its implications, although those involved insisted it was explained to him. The bottom line was that
with state revenues climbing by $5 billion, the schools were entitled
to get the lion's share of that amount. They would get $4.7 billion,
leaving just $300 million for growth in every other state program—
from welfare and health care for the poor to prisons, universities,
and environmental protection. In reality, that would mean deep cuts
in those programs, because they all needed more money to keep up
with expanding caseloads and increasing costs. Schwarzenegger
would need billions more in tax revenue to keep those programs
whole. He concluded that he could keep his deal with the schools
only if he violated another pledge he had made to the voters: that he
would not raise taxes. He refused to raise taxes. So he broke his
agreement with the educators instead.

Gale Kaufman was at her parents' house in Miami Beach over the Christmas holidays when word leaked out that Schwarzenegger intended to break his deal. Kaufman, a veteran Democratic Party operative who ran legislative campaigns and had made a small fortune managing ballot measure races, could not believe what she was hearing. Kaufman discussed the news in a conference call with representatives of several public employee unions for whom she was a consultant.

"What does he think he's doing?" Kaufman remembered asking the others on the call.[3]

The answer to that question soon became clear, and Kaufman and her union allies swung into action. Funded largely by the teachers union, the labor coalition began airing radio and television ads lambasting the governor for breaking his word. Schwarzenegger's budget provided nearly $3 billion in new money to the schools, an increase of 6 percent from the year before. It was a record level of funding, $362 more per child for every student in kindergarten through 12th grade. But it wasn't as much as the school lobby was expecting. And it wasn't as much as they were due under the agreement they had made with the governor. To cut through the complexities of the budget process, the union coalition in its ads used a simple description of the transaction. The governor, they said, had "borrowed" $2 billion from the schools, and now he was refusing to pay it back. That charge was not technically accurate, but it did capture the essence of the conflict: Schwarzenegger had broken his word. To the children. He was a governor who could not be trusted.

The result was devastating. Most voters who heard the ads never knew that Schwarzenegger was proposing to give the schools far more money than they had received the year before. They assumed instead that he was proposing to cut school budgets. And they were angry that he had gone back on his deal. His approval ratings began to fall. By April, only 40 percent of Californians approved of the way he was handling his job. Only 28 percent liked the way he was handling education issues. That was an ominous number in a state where the schools ranked perennially as one of the voters' highest priorities.

The foundation of Schwarzenegger's political house had just developed a huge crack. But rather than pausing to repair it, the governor pushed ahead with his ambitious plans to build a second story. The result was predictable.

At a time when many voters were questioning his credibility and becoming less likely to accept his leadership, Schwarzenegger demanded that the Legislature pass his far-reaching reform program. He and his advisers would later say that the governor was trying to duplicate the dynamic that had worked so well the year before, when he had threatened to take the workers' compensation issue to the ballot if lawmakers did not pass his bill. He never believed that his new threat would actually lead to a special election and a ballot battle. But this time the Democrats did not fall for his feint. And he was not prepared to respond.

Although he prided himself as an excellent chess player, Schwarzenegger had rushed into this confrontation with no coherent strategy, and his tactics were even worse. With a deadline looming for submitting measures that could qualify in time for a November election, his staff scrambled to come up with proposals that they could put into the ballot measure pipeline. They wrote one themselves—the budget reform—but later dropped it in favor of a second version written by two business lobbyists. They adopted as their own a Republican lawmaker's proposal on pensions that would lead to huge problems for Schwarzenegger. They grabbed a proposal on teacher tenure from an assemblywoman who would later distance herself from the idea. And they endorsed a Republican legislative leader's plan for an independent commission to draw new political boundaries, then dropped that one and backed a second measure written by the Sacramento gadfly who had started the recall election.

All of this produced a chaotic scene in which legislators—and voters—were left in the dark for weeks about just what the governor was actually proposing. Schwarzenegger somehow managed to look uncompromising and indecisive at the same time. His aides blamed much of the confusion on a state law that had been interpreted by an ethics commission to bar the governor from controlling the campaign committee that was preparing the ballot measures. But that explanation was only part of the reason. In truth, Schwarzenegger had moved too quickly and didn't really know where he wanted to go. He was attacking some of the biggest, systemic problems in state government, but he had not prepared the voters sufficiently for what was to come. He had not built a bipartisan base for his proposals, and his aggressive, over-the-top rhetoric set Democratic legislators, their interest group allies, and activists on edge.

As those opponents, led by the public employee unions, continued to attack, Schwarzenegger alternated between retreat and renewed assaults, and the mood in the Capitol darkened. Eventually, any hope of a negotiated settlement disappeared. But Schwarzenegger had backed himself into a corner with his threat to call a special election, and he followed through. Voters who were upset at the fight brewing in Sacramento would now be asked to decide on the governor's three surviving proposals—on the budget, on drawing new district lines, and on changing teacher tenure rules. Later, he would endorse a fourth proposal that had reached the ballot independently from his efforts but with his private consent, an initiative that sought to limit the ability of public sector labor unions to collect political contributions from the paychecks of their members. The governor's backing of that proposal further eroded his relationship with Democrats in the Legislature, who depended on the unions for much of their financial backing.

If his initiatives had a theme, it was that Sacramento's politics and finances needed to be freed from the influence of the public employee unions. That concept was not a perfect fit for the measures he backed, but it was closer than anything else. And it was an idea that had some resonance. Even some Democrats, especially those outside the Legislature, conceded in their private moments that the public employee union grip on state policy was too tight. The teachers unions routinely opposed education reforms that could help the poor. And the prison guards union—the California Correctional Peace Officers Association—had become a hugely powerful organization that represented more than 30,000 officers and won a contract in 2002 that gave the guards raises of 37 percent and more control over the day-to-day affairs of the prisons. In one Public Policy Institute of California poll, 61 percent of Californians agreed with the statement that "political contributions from labor unions have too much influence on candidate elections and ballot initiatives." But few establishment Democrats would join Schwarzenegger in such a campaign, and he never found a way to make the case without sounding vindictive and meanspirited. He tried to wrap the union issue in the middle of a positive-sounding troika for his first three years as governor—"Recover, Reform, Rebuild"—but he never fully explained to the masses why his reforms were necessary in order for him to rebuild the state.

Instead, Schwarzenegger and his aides planned to make the contest a referendum on his leadership—a contest between a popular, engaging governor and the faceless bureaucrats and institutions in state government. And at a state Republican convention in Sacramento in February, he sounded a decidedly partisan note: "They can go ahead and do whatever they want," he said of his Democratic opponents. "The train has left the station, and there (are) three things they can do. One is they can join and then jump on the train. Number two, they can go and stand behind and just wave and be left behind. Or number three, they get in front of the train—and you know what happens then."[4]

Schwarzenegger's Republican faithful roared their approval.

But it was the governor's program that got mangled in a train wreck.

The California Teachers Association led the way. The union levied a surcharge on its members and then used the anticipated windfall as security to mortgage the union headquarters building in Burlingame, near San Francisco International Airport. The result: a $50 million political war chest that the union's leaders could use to fight the governor's initiatives. The prison guards used a special assessment of their own to raise $18 million. Just about every other union in the state joined in. By the time the election was over, Schwarzenegger's opponents had spent nearly $133 million. Schwarzenegger's side spent $56 million, including $8 million from the governor's personal bank account.[5]

More important than the money, though, was what the unions did with it. They devised a campaign message that turned Schwarzenegger's strategy on its head. While he wanted to attack the unions as power-driven special interests with no connection to the people, the unions put some of their members—real people—in television ads attacking the governor. A firefighter, a police officer, a nurse, and a teacher looked into the camera and told voters that Schwarzenegger was a power-hungry bully doing the bidding of big business.

In one version of the ad, the commercial opened with famous shots of Schwarzenegger announcing for governor two years before on Jay Leno's show. "I do not have to bow to any special interests," Schwarzenegger said in the clip. "I have plenty of money. No one can pay me off. Trust me." At that point a firefighter appeared on the screen. "But now he's taking millions from developers and big business," he said. Cut to police officer standing in front of his car. "And pushing their agenda with his special election."

Another featured a one-time teacher of the year in a simple setting speaking directly to the camera. "Keeping your word," said teacher Liane Cismowski. "It's a cherished principle we teach our students. So how can Governor Schwarzenegger break his promise?"[6]

The strategy worked. Schwarzenegger's approval ratings kept dropping, his ballot measures started falling behind, and they never caught up. The governor opened last-minute negotiations with Assembly Speaker Fabian Núñez to see if he could salvage some face-saving compromises by canceling, or postponing, the election. But the attack on the unions had taken its toll, and with some on his own staff arguing against a compromise, the talks fell apart.

The results on Election Day were ugly. The voters defeated all of the measures Schwarzenegger was backing, some by huge margins. The budget reform lost by 62 to 38. The measure on new districts lost by 60 to 40. The teacher tenure proposal went down 55 to 45. Ironically, the most partisan of the measures, the one to restrict the use of union dues for political activity, lost by the narrowest margin of the four. It was defeated 53.5 to 46.5.

Schwarzenegger's approval rating also took a beating. By the time of the election, only 33 percent of voters approved of his performance. And just 36 percent said they would be inclined to elect him to a second term. As a politician, he was reeling. Battered, bruised, and in debt, he was an unpopular Republican facing a re-election campaign in a Democratic state in a year that was already shaping up nationally to be favorable to Democrats. But having taken his punishment, Schwarzenegger still had time on his side.

He also had a secret weapon that few of his opponents believed he could wield to such great advantage: humility.

SEVEN

Lessons Learned

After his debacle at the polls in 2005, Schwarzenegger had to decide quickly how to react. He could have blamed his loss on the public employee unions that spent more than $100 million to defeat his measures. He could have lashed out at the voters for being swayed by the ads the unions aired. He certainly could have wondered what happened to the Republican base that failed to show up for a slate of ballot measures that had been widely portrayed as a partisan jihad.

But none of that would have been particularly productive, nor would it have helped heal the wounds that his bitter campaign had opened. What he needed was a clean break, a new start, a dramatic way to convince voters that he had received their message.

Schwarzenegger chose a route that few politicians travel, but more probably should: he took full and complete responsibility for what had happened. He admitted his mistakes. And he didn't just own up to his misdeeds once, with muddled language in muffled tones muttered under his breath. He embraced the topic of his political redemption with all the zeal he had thrown into the campaign the year before. He was like a man in therapy, trying to work through his errors and make amends with each and every person he had wronged.

One thing Schwarzenegger did not do was apologize for the ideas he had pursued in the special election. He stood by them, and has ever since—to the consternation of those on the left who demanded that he renounce his agenda. What he said was that his approach to enacting that agenda was wrong. He had moved too quickly, consulted too little, and pushed on the voters a special election that they did not want.

"I think that I operate with a different mentality than most people do, which is that I am very forceful and impatient," Schwarzenegger told reporters two days after the special election.[1] "I always have mapped out, my entire life, a program and a work schedule, and also a schedule of when I want to accomplish things, and I always was successful with that, and with tremendous determination and with a tremendous amount of will."

He compared his approach while governing California to that of an executive taking over a company in bankruptcy. "There are certain things you have to do," he said. In his first year, he put in place the framework for fiscal recovery, restructuring the state's debt and slowing the growth in spending. That had stopped the bleeding and stabilized the situation. In his second year, he had hoped to reform state government to prepare it for bigger change to come. He thought he needed those reforms in order to launch a program to rebuild the state's aging infrastructure.

"And so I said, 'Okay, second year, reform.' Well, the legislators, they don't want to go along with my reforms, so I'm going to go out and gather signatures. That will signal a message to them, maybe that will bring them to the table. . . . And then it didn't happen, and they did not respond. So then I said, 'Okay, then we're going to go and call a special election.' And so this is how we moved forward, but it was with this same determination."

What he learned is that government and politics do not work well with rigid timelines, and an executive in a democracy cannot will his way to action like the CEO of a major corporation. A governor in a state as large as California can barely control his own sprawling bureaucracy, a workforce of more than 200,000, let alone the other branches of government. He cannot hire and fire the 120 legislators. They are independently elected by the same people who put him into office. He has to work with them to get anything done, even if they approach the job from a world view entirely different from his own.

As a passionate advocate of direct democracy, Schwarzenegger had no choice but to accept the results. They showed that the voters did not want his ideas, not in the form he presented them, nor in the way he went about trying to enact his agenda. Even if he clung to the principles that his measures embodied, he would have to put them on the shelf, retool, and approach them in a different way. He compared the outcome to a lousy box office for one of his movies.

"I've always relied on the people, and I always listened very carefully to the people," he said. "And that's something that you have to do when you're in the movie business, you have to listen carefully to the people. If one of the movies goes in the toilet, you know that was the wrong story, that's not the kind of movie you want to do. So you then change and you learn from that. And so I've learned from that, that the people sent a message to us that, 'Don't come to us with all your stuff. . . . Work it out at the Capitol.' And so that's exactly what we're going to do."[2]

A few weeks later, in his annual state of the state speech to the Legislature, in the ornate, refurbished chambers of the California Assembly, Schwarzenegger elaborated. "I have absorbed my defeat," he told lawmakers. "I have learned my lesson. And the people, who always have the last word, sent a clear message: cut the warfare, cool the rhetoric, find common ground and fix the problems together. To my fellow Californians, I say—message received."

This was strong and effective language. He might have been talking to the legislators in the room that night, but he was speaking directly to the voters and acknowledging their power. He was, in effect, giving them a rationale for supporting his reelection, even if they didn't realize it yet. By defeating his measures, he was saying, they had helped him find a better way, and now he was going to change in response to their will. He was going to be more collaborative, less confrontational. In making his transformation so bold, and so open, he invited criticism from political insiders. But he also gave the voters a reason to want him to do well. Reelecting him, making him a success again, would be proof that their votes mattered. He was validating their judgment. It might have been perverse logic. But it worked.

The change, moreover, was not only for public consumption. After some reflection, Schwarzenegger realized that he needed to abandon the caricature of himself that he had carried into the governor's office from Hollywood. No more name-calling. No more stunts laden with special effects—smashed up cars and giant faucets spewing red ink. There would be very few references to his movies in his speeches anymore, and usually only to poke fun at himself. He was, after all, still a world-famous action movie star. He still had the ability to stir a crowd simply by showing up. He could build on that advantage by speaking on substantive issues at some length to real audiences in public forums. The result—hearing the man previously known as "The Terminator" speaking seriously about public policy—was more jarring, and more effective, than when Schwarzenegger was playing strictly to type.

"I figured out after the 2005 special election that I have taken the wrong approach by being too pushy, by being personal about things and attacking people and saying 'girly men' and all of those things," Schwarzenegger said later.[3] "That didn't move the agenda forward, but that was my way of expressing myself then. I didn't know any better. If I would have known any better I wouldn't have done it. And then I've learned that there's a better way and that is to bring people together, not to insult them, but to actually bring the best out of people, bring the best out of Democrats, bring the best out of Republicans."

And so, even as the rest of the country was moving into a bitterly divisive election year in 2006, Schwarzenegger was leading California into relative political harmony. He still had a partisan election of his own to manage, but inside the Capitol, he was determined to work across party lines to build a solid record of accomplishment. He wanted not just to be governor, but to actually govern.

As he reached out to the center and the left, however, Schwarzenegger immediately found himself in trouble with the right. Republican activists, who in California tend to be very conservative, were appalled at his renewed willingness to do business with the opposition. They rose up in near revolt after he hired a Democrat, Susan Kennedy, to be his new chief of staff. But what many of them did not realize at first was that Kennedy had evolved into an ideological hybrid herself, like her new boss. She was as disgusted as he was with the power the public employee unions wielded over her fellow Democrats. And as a member of the state's Public Utilities Commission, she had built a reputation as a hard-nosed advocate for open markets and competition. Kennedy's decision to work for Schwarzenegger was a defection from the Democrats. A smart, driven, top-ranking operative in the Democratic Party was going to serve a Republican governor. She set out to help him govern more effectively so that he could win reelection, even as many of her former colleagues shunned her.

"It was easier for me to come out as gay than it was to admit that I was a Democrat for Schwarzenegger," she said.[4]

But rather than seeing Kennedy's hiring as a coup for Schwarzenegger, Republicans turned the episode upside down. They saw it as Schwarzenegger capitulating to his opponents. And they expected the worst.

Jon Fleischman, a former executive director of the state Republican Party, had recently started a web log that had become an overnight sensation among conservative activists. Fleischman used the blog to report insider gossip, assess policy proposals, and

pressure elected officials to follow the party line. And when
Schwarzenegger hired Kennedy, Fleischman led the attack.

"While Republicans are not a majority in California by a long
shot, there are still many millions of us out here," he wrote. "It
doesn't seem plausible that there was not one person who could
ably serve in this capacity who agrees with the governor's general
philosophy enough to register in the same political party as he
does."[5]

But if the Kennedy hiring flummoxed insiders, they were even
more confused when Schwarzenegger began to assemble the staff
that would manage his reelection campaign, and appeared to be tacking back to the right. Maria Shriver—a liberal Democrat herself—
led the search, but it was a quest that ended in an unexpected
place: the Bush White House. Shriver recommended that Schwarzenegger hire two men—Matthew Dowd and Steve Schmidt—who
had been top aides to Bush and Vice President Dick Cheney. Dowd
had worked for Democrats before joining Bush when he was governing Texas in a bipartisan fashion. He helped run the 2000 campaign and then was senior strategist for the hyper-partisan 2004
reelection effort. That campaign, while ultimately successful, had
soured him on the divisive state of modern politics in America, and
Dowd was eager to work again for a candidate whose message
could cross traditional party boundaries.

Although Bush and Cheney and anyone so closely associated
with them were radioactive in liberal circles, Shriver said she wasn't
bothered by the connection. "They're the best at what they do," she
said flatly when asked why she recruited the two Bush Republicans
to help her husband win in a Democratic state. "I was looking for
people who understood communication. . . . They both listened.
They're not dogmatic. Both knew California. I think that's always
helpful. But I think if you've run a presidential campaign, you know
how to run a campaign, and if you think strategically and holisti-
cally, like Matthew does, you know about how to communicate."[6]

The resulting stew was unique in recent American politics. Schwarzenegger was a moderate Republican governor with a Democratic chief of staff and a campaign team headed by veterans of one of the most aggressively partisan Republican presidential political operations in American history. The fact that they worked almost seamlessly together was not only a testament to Schwarzenegger's ability to meld left and right. It also showed that, by 2006, he felt more comfortable setting the agenda and hiring people to pursue it than he did running with a script that others developed and handed to him based on their interpretation of what he wanted to do.

Kennedy, Dowd, and Schmidt all knew that to win a second term, Schwarzenegger was first going to have to show more results from his first three years in office. And to do that, he was going to have to compromise. His Republican allies simply did not have the votes to enact their own agenda. He could rail against the Democrats, refuse to budge, and get nothing done, but that would have probably meant losing the election. Or he could work with them.

On the wall in her office, Kennedy tacked a list she called the "coalition of the pissed." It included all the interest groups that were mad at Schwarzenegger, not just for his policies but for the way they had been treated by him and his staff. There were the obvious ones, like the teachers union and the prison guards. But the list also included some erstwhile allies, such as the California Manufacturers and Technology Association. She reached out to all of them—not necessarily promising to satisfy their demands but at least making them feel as if they were being heard in the governor's office again.

Schwarzenegger did make some concessions in the months that followed. Despite higher tax revenues, his new budget made little progress in erasing the troublesome gap between the money coming into state government and the money going out. Instead of making cuts, his budget for 2006–7 spent $8 billion more than the state was taking in from taxes that year. It was like blowing an entire Christmas bonus when there were still credit cards to pay and the monthly budget showed more expenses than income. The top goal on which he ran in 2003—getting the state's finances back in order—would have to wait until his second term.

Schwarzenegger also signed a bill to increase the state's minimum wage, a move he had once opposed. He had vetoed a measure to raise the minimum in 2005. But at the time he said that he would be happy to sign such a bill if Democrats dropped their insistence on an automatic, annual cost-of-living increase in the wage. At first, the Democrats resisted. Some of them thought they could get him to sign the bill they wanted. Others did not want to let him take credit in an election year for increasing the wage. But after Schwarzenegger took steps to raise the minimum without a vote of the Legislature, through a state commission that had the power to review and adjust the minimum wage, Democrats relented. They sent him a bill that raised the wage by $1.25 over two years without an annual cost-of-living increase, and he signed it.

Schwarzenegger's biggest concession to election-year politics was on the issue of prescription drug discounts. Since his first days as governor, Schwarzenegger had been trying to work on a plan that would encourage the pharmaceutical companies to offer discounts to low- and middle-income Californians. He had insisted at first that the plan be voluntary for the drug companies. When Democrats put a measure on the ballot to force the industry to comply or risk losing their lucrative contracts to sell billions of dollars in drugs to the plan that cared for California's poor, he opposed it. But in 2006, he abandoned his resistance to mandatory discounts and signed a bill that Big Pharma opposed. His staff portrayed it as a compromise, and it did have elements from both approaches. But it was mostly a capitulation by Schwarzenegger to the demands of the Democrats and consumer groups.

As he cut these deals and negotiated with the Legislature on two bigger issues—a massive package of public works bonds and a bill to enact the nation's first cap on greenhouse gases— Schwarzenegger began to see that partisan sentiments in the Capitol were not an accurate reflection of public opinion in the state. The loudest activists in the parties, the ones who control the party organizations and get quoted in the media, tend to be the ideological purists. In contrast, people who consider them- selves Republicans or Democrats but are not political junkies, who don't attend conventions or march in the streets, tend to be far more pragmatic. In California, in 2006, polls showed that while Schwarzenegger might have been angering the most conservative part of his base, his actions were in line with what mainstream Republicans, independents, and many Democrats wanted out of state government.

In the Capitol, he had a hard time rounding up Republican votes for his policy measures. It seemed at times as if the working defini- tion of bipartisanship was 41 Democrats in the Assembly and 21 in the Senate—the number of lawmakers it took to pass a bill—plus Schwarzenegger. But Schwarzenegger was looking beyond the Capitol's right-leaning Republican lawmakers to the broader Republican electorate, and there he found his support much deeper and broader. His conception of bipartisanship, or, later, postparti- sanship, did not end at the Capitol's heavy oaken doors.

By steadily working his way back to the center, and by getting things done, Schwarzenegger began to rehabilitate his relationship with the voters. Then he got lucky. In June of 2006, the Democrats, after a bitter primary, chose as their nominee to run against him the state's treasurer, Phil Angelides. Smart, articulate, and driven, Angelides was a prickly former chairman of the state Democratic Party who had become more openly liberal and stridently partisan the longer he was in office. Once Schwarzenegger took over after the recall, Angelides was almost alone among Democratic office- holders in refusing to work with him. Opposing everything

Schwarzenegger proposed, he described himself as the "anti-Arnold." He had even raised money to pay for a few television commercials attacking Schwarzenegger's first budget plan. And as he prepared to run for governor, Angelides chided Schwarzenegger for refusing to raise taxes, and he promised to raise taxes on the wealthy and on business if he became governor. Although Angelides was a millionaire himself, he tried to use middle-class resentment of the wealthy as a tool to defeat the governor.

In his announcement speech, Angelides talked of his family to draw a contrast with Schwarzenegger, implying that the governor's public service was only an excuse to feed his ego. Angelides said his father did not attend the University of California to "glorify himself." And his parents did not work all their lives to "drive fancy cars or see their names on a marquee." He added: "We have a governor who thinks it's fine to cut assistance to children, to the poor—that somehow, if we just shower more fortune on the fortunate, the crumbs will reach the rest, like leftovers of a Hollywood dinner party." Schwarzenegger, the Democrat said, believed that life was like an "athletic endurance contest, where only the strong should survive, where we just lavish more on those who have the most."[7]

Angelides' image as an angry partisan made him probably the least popular major party nominee for governor in the state's history. Just before the primary election, only 27 percent of likely general election voters—and just 24 percent of independents—said they had a favorable impression of Angelides. Yet once he won the nomination, Angelides made almost no effort to appeal to the center, and little attempt to engage Schwarzenegger or the voters in a serious discussion about the future of the state. Instead, his strategy was mainly to link Schwarzenegger to President Bush. The Democrat's campaign grasped at straws, railing at Schwarzenegger one day for failing to renounce his rejected reforms, on another for referring in private to a Republican assemblywoman, a Latina, as "hot-blooded." That comment was captured on a recording made by Schwarzenegger's speechwriter and inadvertently left on a loosely protected public website, where Angelides researchers discovered it and leaked it to a reporter. In another bizarre moment, a senior adviser to Angelides suggested to reporters that two of Schwarzenegger's campaign aides were about to be summoned to testify in the Washington, D.C., trial of White House aide Scooter Libby. They never were—but nothing else he tried seemed to work. Barely a year after voters had rejected the governor's agenda at the polls, they increasingly saw the incumbent as a moderate centrist and his opponent as a stubborn liberal.

Schwarzenegger's campaign, meanwhile, was almost understated, compared with the slash-and-burn style he had shown in 2003 and 2005. His main appeal to partisanship was an unfair portrayal of Angelides' tax proposals. Schwarzenegger's campaign not only exaggerated them—telling voters that the Democrat planned to hike taxes by $18 billion when the real total was perhaps one-fourth of that—but it did so even as the governor refused to explain how he would balance the budget without raising taxes. The Schwarzenegger camp also painted the Democrat's proposal for expanding health care as a massive tax increase that would cripple the economy. Meanwhile, behind closed doors, Schwarzenegger's aides were writing a plan for him that would be even more expensive. The campaign's favorite advertising technique was an image of Angelides appearing to walk backward as an announcer warned that the Democrat would undo all the progress the state was making under Schwarzenegger. The governor's positive ads were in the style of those image-building corporate commercials that try to make the viewer feel good but don't mention the sponsor until the very end. The ads were filled with beautiful pictures of the California coast, its cities, the Central Valley's verdant heartland, and the Sierra, but hardly any glimpses of Schwarzenegger himself.

His campaign's skill and discipline, his renewed collaboration with the Legislature, and his opponent's decision to appeal mainly to Democrats all served to make possible a Schwarzenegger victory— an outcome that only a few months earlier had seemed far-fetched.

But all of that might have been insufficient without two major accomplishments that put Schwarzenegger on the national stage as a different kind of Republican and cemented his ties with independent voters.

EIGHT

Cranes

In late August of 2006, as the rest of the country was entering the home stretch of a bitterly partisan election year, Schwarzenegger was campaigning in Del Mar, a wealthy little burg on the San Diego County coast. His appearance there typified the ideological jumble that his administration had come to represent: He was a Republican governor talking to an audience of African-American entrepreneurs about a topic that crossed party lines.

Schwarzenegger urged the members of the California Black Chamber of Commerce to support more than $37 billion in public works bonds he had pushed the Legislature to place on the ballot, easily the largest single package of borrowing ever contemplated by a state government. "If this passes in November, we're going to start rebuilding California," Schwarzenegger said. "There will be cranes everywhere. We will be laying cement. We will be laying steel. There will be action everywhere."[1]

That sort of exuberance for growth and public works had not been heard in California for at least a generation, perhaps not since Democrat Edmund G. Brown was governor and cheering the Golden State's emergence ahead of New York as the most populous state in the union. In the interim, many Californians, themselves newcomers or the children of newcomers who arrived in the years after World War II, had ceased to celebrate the state's relentless growth. Instead, they became famous for pulling up the drawbridge shortly after their arrival. Complaining about traffic, overcrowded schools, and pollution, they adopted a patchwork of local ballot measures limiting growth so that the next wave of migrants from other states or abroad could not do what they had done. In one poll taken on the subject in 2006, just 12 percent of California voters thought the growth expected by 2025 would be a good thing, while 60 percent said it would be bad for the state.

Schwarzenegger, though, was not embarrassed to be enthusiastic about growth, which he had always equated with progress, and he was eager to be seen as a governor who did not shrink from the challenge it provided. He could have focused in public only on the part of his program designed to catch up with the services needed for people already in the state. Instead, he conflated their needs with his desire to prepare for the millions more who were still coming, a politically risky message since those millions, having not yet arrived, would have no say in the matter when his proposals were put to a vote.

"We will be building more highways, more freeways, more tunnels, more bridges," Schwarzenegger told the black business owners. "We will be modernizing 100,000 classrooms. We will be building more schools, expanding our university system, expanding our community colleges, all of those things."

He was starting to sound like a Democrat. But then came the clincher. If the bonds passed, he said, "We will need a lot of workers and need a lot of companies, and so we will need everyone to work to get the job done. If it's big businesses, small businesses, women-owned businesses, minority-owned businesses—everyone will have to work together on this."

With that line Schwarzenegger tied the whole thing together. His vision for rebuilding California, he was saying, was something that men and women, business and labor, white, Latino, Asian, and black could all support without worrying about party politics. To even get on the ballot, the proposals had required the backing of two-thirds of the members of the Legislature, which meant that the package needed considerable support from Democrats and Republicans alike. He wasn't talking just about bricks and mortar. He was preaching unity. The only serious opposition to the proposals came from conservative anti-tax groups worried that the debt service on the bonds would eventually lead to higher taxes.

Schwarzenegger had been talking about infrastructure since 2005, when he tried to sell his failed government and political reform package as a necessary step in his plan to "reform, then rebuild" California. But rather than retreat after voters rejected his slate of ballot measures, he moved forward with a bigger public works plan than anyone in the Capitol expected. A year before a freeway bridge collapse in Minnesota prompted a national conversation on the country's infrastructure deficit, Schwarzenegger had seized the issue as his own and was preaching the virtues of investing in highways, schools, and levees in California.

It was sound policy. But by proposing a bigger, more dramatic package than anyone imagined he would, Schwarzenegger also devised a brilliant political strategy that changed the entire tone of debate in the state. The Legislature might easily have ignored a more modest plan, which could have been lost in the usual shuffle of election-year proposals. But the program Schwarzenegger offered was so big, so audacious, that it came to dominate the political discussion and even seep into the consciousness of Californians who were not absorbed in politics.

"It gave him something to talk about that was so organically his that it lit him on fire," said his chief of staff, Susan Kennedy. "The timing was right, we knew it was the right thing to do, and it put him at the center of an issue that drew everyone to the same table."[2]

Schwarzenegger outlined his plan and his argument for it in a speech to the Legislature on January 5, 2006. The state, he said, had for too long neglected to invest in the highways, streets, schools, levees, prisons, and other public facilities needed to serve a growing population that had reached 37 million by 2006. And now California was facing a projected population increase of as much as 30 percent over 20 years—the equivalent of adding three new cities the size of Los Angeles.

"Our systems are at the breaking point now," Schwarzenegger said. "We need more roads, more hospitals, more schools, more nurses, more teachers, more police, more fire, more water, more energy, more ports . . . more, more, more.

"But we cannot be overwhelmed by this reality. We cannot freeze in the face of this future. We cannot bury our head in the sand and say—if we don't build it, they won't come."

The "strategic growth plan" Schwarzenegger proposed would cost $222 billion over 10 years, with $68 billion of that coming from bond measures—borrowed money—and the rest representing the flow of existing state and federal taxes and anticipated investment by the private sector. It did not include any new taxes, in spite of his sweeping description of the state's needs and what was at stake.

The plan called for adding 1,200 miles of new highway and carpool lanes and 600 miles of mass transit, which he promised would actually reduce traffic delays over the following 10 years even as the state's population continued to grow. It called for spending more money on transportation projects specifically targeted toward reducing air pollution.

He proposed building more than 2,000 new schools and 40,000 classrooms while modernizing another 140,000. To prepare for a half million new college students, he proposed more classrooms, libraries, and science labs in hundreds of new university buildings across the state.

The state's water supply, he said, had barely been expanded in 50 years, and, since the Hurricane Katrina disaster in New Orleans, California's system of levees and dikes had been exposed as the most vulnerable in the nation. He wanted to fix it.

Local jails and state prisons were so overcrowded that criminals were being released early or left on the street "because we have no room to lock them up," Schwarzenegger said. He proposed two new prisons, a new crime lab, emergency response facilities, and space for 83,000 new prisoners. He also asked for 101 new courts, 56 renovations, and 44 expansions to help deal with a growing backlog of cases.

His program was not embraced by everyone. On the right, conservatives blanched at the borrowing he was proposing, and his talk of wanting "more" of everything sounded like fingernails on a blackboard to their ears. Republican Party activists denounced the plan, and a movement began to get the party to oppose it officially at its next statewide convention. Schwarzenegger's allies eventually beat down the rebellion, but they never persuaded fiscal conservatives to endorse his program.

On the left, the state's treasurer, Phil Angelides, who was running for the Democratic nomination for governor, accused Schwarzenegger of exaggerating the impact his proposals would have on the state's backlog of public works projects. Angelides noted that California's voters had approved an average of about $7.1 billion a year in bonds over the previous five years, and the governor's package offered $68 billion over 10 years, or $6.8 billion a year.

"We need to do more than we are doing," Angelides said. "The governor's plan is full of a lot of hype and has numbers that don't tell the truth."[3]

Angelides correctly described the numbers in Schwarzenegger's plan, and he was right that the governor's program was neither as coherent nor as forward-looking as it could have been. But Schwarzenegger's proposal was unique in that he was offering a 10-year program of capital projects based on what he concluded were the state's long-term needs, not the sort of random, moment-to-moment decision making—including ballot measures proposed by initiative—that had produced the other recent bonds to which Angelides was referring. Schwarzenegger's "hype" was the governor's way of getting the voters interested in a subject that might otherwise make their eyes glaze over. His showmanship connected the public's frustration over crumbling infrastructure with a government program designed to address it.

That strategy worked. Among mainstream Californians, the package was definitely a hit. In a Public Policy Institute of California poll in March 2006, a remarkable 69 percent of California adults, including 75 percent of Republicans, said they supported the governor's plan. Even when they were asked explicitly about the proposed borrowing, 59 percent of Republicans said they supported it, as did 54 percent of Democrats and 53 percent of independents. Support for the proposal was spread evenly across the state. For people stuck in daily traffic jams in the San Francisco Bay Area or sending their children to broken-down public schools in South-Central Los Angeles or overcrowded universities in San Diego, these proposals were more real than any abstract concern about debt service or proper long-range planning. And although Republican lawmakers might not have been happy, Republican voters seemed to like the plan even more than Democrats did. A Democratic governor could not have done as well because Republican voters almost certainly would have opposed the massive package of borrowing had it originated on the left.

The Democrats who controlled the Legislature signaled that they were open to working with Schwarzenegger but wanted to put their imprint on the final package. They certainly had the leverage to do so. If the governor wanted his proposals on the ballot, he would need the cooperation of the Democrats, because his failures the year before had made the initiative process no longer an option. And since he had far more at stake politically than did the Democrats, he would have to defer to their wishes in many cases. If not, they could simply walk away from the table and likely not suffer any consequences at the polls, while he would be left looking weak and ineffective just as he was heading into his campaign for a second term. Somehow, he would have to respond to Democratic demands while also building enough support from Republicans to secure the two-thirds majority necessary to win passage in the Legislature. That would not be an easy task.

Schwarzenegger also had to deal with the personal needs of the legislative leaders, including some sensitive egos. The Senate's leader, Don Perata of Oakland, had been pushing a big transportation bond for more than a year that had received little attention in the media. Now that Schwarzenegger had jumped on board and upped the ante, the governor was getting all the press and Perata appeared to resent it. The senator established his own campaign committee to raise money and promote the cause, which he called the "Perata Plan," and he made it clear that Schwarzenegger would have to deal with his concerns if he wanted to get anything on the ballot.

In an interview with the *Sacramento Bee*, Perata noted that he and Schwarzenegger were like two men driving in a car.[4] When they arrived at their destination, he predicted, Schwarzenegger would jump out and be mobbed by the public and press. He was the celebrity, after all.

"I go park the car," Perata said, sounding self-deprecating. Then he added: "But I am driving the car." His point was obvious enough. Schwarzenegger might get all the credit. But watch the details to see who was really getting what they wanted.

What the Democrats wanted was to shrink Schwarzenegger's overall package while also substituting their priorities for his own. They wanted less money for highways, for example, and more for transit. They wanted less for building new schools and more for renovating old ones. They did not want any new dams but wanted to spend more money on improving water quality and buying open space for animal habitat. They did not want any prison bonds or

money for new courthouses. And they proposed adding an entirely
new bond to pay for housing for the poor. In short, their desires reflected the needs of their more urban, low-income constituency,
and not the demands of the state's fast-growing suburban (and
largely Republican) communities.

Republican lawmakers did agree with Democrats about one
thing: the entire package would have to be smaller than Schwarzenegger was proposing. But they largely supported the policy
choices reflected in the governor's proposals. They also wanted to
use the opportunity to overhaul the state's environmental laws to
reduce regulation on new construction. And they wanted a "pay-as-
you-go" element that would commit a certain percentage of the
state's budget to infrastructure every year so that the state could
build more public works while borrowing less. Because the bonds
required a two-thirds majority in each house of the Legislature to
get on the ballot, the Republicans had some leverage. But they
could push Schwarzenegger only so far, or the Democrats would
abandon the negotiations and leave the governor twisting in the
wind.

That, in fact, is almost what happened. The differences between
the parties, and among the majority Democrats, produced a stalemate that threatened to unravel the entire package. As the deadline
for placing the bonds on the June ballot approached, each house of
the Legislature passed a piece of the program, but neither house
approved the other's action. Schwarzenegger blamed the Senate's
Democratic leader and his fellow Republicans for the failure.

"Perata is trying to derail everything," Schwarzenegger told his
chief speechwriter in a private conversation, according to a transcript that was later made public. "He's still fuming, and he's trying
to be an obstructionist. . . . Perata is a very sick man."

Republican lawmakers, for their part, were being small-minded,
Schwarzenegger said. They asked him what was in it for them and
their constituents, rather than thinking of the state as a whole, and

they complained that the package did not include enough of the reforms they had called for. In a bit of grandiosity, he compared the job ahead of him to JFK's task of building support for sending a man to the moon.

"I said, 'Now is when we have a chance here, and you want to have it all perfect,'" Schwarzenegger told his aide, recounting his conversation with Republican legislators. "'It won't happen. You're not the majority.' I said, 'When does that get into your mind? You're not the majority. This is a great opportunity. Is it perfect? No. But it's a great opportunity for us to move forward and do something big, and to get us on a roll that we are building California. This creates unbelievable optimism in California. Everyone likes to do it. So don't start nitpicking here.'"

But Schwarzenegger was also at fault. He sent mixed signals about whether he wanted the bonds on the June ballot or in November. He first insisted on getting his entire package, and then suggested he would be satisfied with only part of it. And he tried to engage in serial negotiations with the legislative leaders. As he would approach a deal with one of them, one or more of the others would object to the details. He could never seem to get them all on the same page.

After the deal fell apart, the reaction was swift, and predictable. Political pundits saw the collapse of the negotiations as a blow to Schwarzenegger's political comeback and predicted that voters would hold him responsible. The Democratic candidates took a break from fighting each other to take swipes at the governor. "I think voters are seeing each and every day that this governor just doesn't have the competence and the credibility to govern," Angelides said.[5] "He doesn't have the ability to do the hard work of moving the state forward." The other Democrat in the race, Controller Steve Westly, echoed those comments. "This is a deeply troubling failure of leadership," Westly, who had once worked closely with Schwarzenegger, said in a statement released by his

campaign. "Future generations will suffer because of it. It's clear
the governor has lost the support of both Democrats and
Republicans. It's clear he needs to go."[6]

That kind of attack would have continued until Election Day
had Schwarzenegger not salvaged the package. But he shrugged off
the temporary setback and, with his usual optimism, insisted that
everything would work out in the end. In fact, the delay might have
helped him. Rather than putting the bonds on the June primary ballot, where the Democratic candidates might have felt compelled to
oppose the package, he was now in position to place the program
on the November ballot, when voters would also be deciding his
fate. He wouldn't have the accomplishment under his belt the way
he would have had the proposals passed in June. But if he could get
the package through the Legislature, he would have evidence that
he could make bipartisan peace with lawmakers. And he would be
campaigning with Democratic leaders and their allies on behalf of
his proposals at the same time his Democratic opponent was trying
to portray him as a partisan zealot.

To reach that result, Schwarzenegger did something that ran
against his instincts. He removed himself from the public debate
over the details of the package, and asked the legislative leaders
from both parties to sit down with each other and work it out. The
governor's office remained involved, with Schwarzenegger's staff
telling legislators and their aides what the governor could accept
and where he would not go. But the tactic forced the Democratic
leaders, Perata and Núñez, to resolve their differences and stop
blaming Schwarzenegger. And it compelled the Republican leaders
to engage in the negotiations in a way that would give them buy-in
at the end.

The turning point probably came when a coalition of environmental groups qualified for the ballot an initiative proposing a $5.4
billion bond for water quality, ocean protection, parks, and habitat.
That measure took those issues off the table in the Legislature.

And with Democrats no longer pushing for a water and parks measure, Republicans lost the leverage they needed to demand that new dams be included. Removing that bitter argument over water storage allowed the party leaders to work on other issues about which there was far more common ground. And they soon reached agreement.

Although the final package was about half the size of the total program Schwarzenegger had originally proposed, it was far larger than the one the governor had requested for the first phase of his plan. And although Republican activists continued to grumble about the price tag, Republican lawmakers won several concessions that made the package truly bipartisan. The Democrats got the money for public transit they wanted, for example, but Republicans won even more for roads than Schwarzenegger was originally seeking. Republicans also insisted that one of their pet projects—improvements to Highway 99, which runs down the spine of the nation's most fertile agricultural valley—be guaranteed $1 billion; it was the only specific earmark in the entire transportation package. Another piece of the package locked in part of the state sales tax for transportation construction, giving Republicans a portion of the "pay-as-you-go" strategy that they insisted be a complement to any more debt. And two bills that accompanied the bonds allowed for a speedy environmental review of certain transportation projects and waived the California Environmental Quality Act, the state's landmark environmental law, for the levee repair projects. None of these details were as sexy as the $37 billion price tag on the bonds, but they were important concessions that balanced the overall agreement more in favor of Republican principles than the party's conservative activists gave it credit for.

The package was supported not only by the governor and the four legislative leaders, but also by both U.S. senators from California and all of the state's constitutional officers. It was backed by the Chamber of Commerce and the Business Round-table. The California Teachers Association, which had spent $50 million defeating Schwarzenegger's initiatives the year before, spent $5 million to help pass the education bond in 2006. Builders, farmers, and trade unions all backed the package.

"California is in desperate need for modern infrastructure improvements," Senator Feinstein, the state's senior elected Democrat, said at one rally for the bonds. "Our schools are overcrowded, our roads and highways are deteriorating and are jammed with traffic, and our protection from catastrophic floods due to levee failure is seriously lacking."[7]

A majority of voters agreed. The bonds passed with between 57 percent and 64 percent of the vote. The flood control bonds pulled in the largest majority, a strong expression of statewide unity, since the levee projects those bonds would pay for would provide only an indirect benefit to vote-rich Southern California, which supported them nonetheless.

The next day, Schwarzenegger said he was "over the moon" with pleasure at the result. "The reason I think they were successful was because Democrats and Republicans worked together," Schwarzenegger said. "It was because the people saw that we are working together, that we were able, bringing both of the parties together, and accomplishing all the things that we have accomplished in the last three years. . . . I think this was also the message we have gotten yesterday from the people by their vote, is, you know, they're saying they want us to continue working this way. This was not a vote just for me or for any particular party. . . . This was basically them letting us know that we need to go in that same direction, which is bringing both of the parties together and moving California forward and making decisions of what is best for the state of California."[8]

Californians might not have shared their governor's optimism, but they bought into his vision. Schwarzenegger's infrastructure package had come to represent more than the sum of its parts. It wasn't only about roads and trains and schools. It was a statement about collaboration and cooperation, about bipartisanship and what the government could accomplish when politicians worked together and interest groups accepted compromise instead of only tolerating all-out victory. The size of the package was itself re-markable as an investment in the future of the state. But the unity of purpose it represented was even more extraordinary in an age of divisive partisan politics.

NINE

Jolly Green Governor

It was hard to take Schwarzenegger seriously in the summer of 2003 when, running for governor the first time, he appeared on a bluff overlooking a Santa Barbara beach to outline the environmental program he promised to pursue if he won. He was, after all, the man who had encouraged General Motors to convert the Humvee from a military vehicle into a consumer product, a massive, diesel-powered all-terrain vehicle that became an emblem for wasteful petroleum consumption and pollution. He admitted he had known little about the environmental policies he was proposing until he decided to run a few weeks before. And when pressed about the details of his plan, he could answer few questions from reporters who attended the event.

"This is a charade," said Pedro Nava, a member of the state Coastal Commission who came to protest. "This guy has no environmental background or history. . . . You just don't wake up one morning and decide you're an environmentalist."[1]

Unless you are Arnold Schwarzenegger. That is exactly what he did. And then he went on to make the issue the marquee subject of his first term as governor. His stands on the environment—in favor of aggressive government action designed to protect it—helped define him as a different kind of Republican, and they eventually propelled him onto the covers of national magazines and the international political stage. By the time he stood for reelection in 2006, polls showed that California voters trusted Schwarzenegger more than his Democratic opponent on the environment.

Schwarzenegger's environmental advocacy, moreover, did not stop at the state's borders. He helped persuade several other states to join California in the fight against global warming, and his prominence on the issue led the way for Republican candidates for president to move to the center as well. Schwarzenegger, sometimes to the frustration of California's Democrats, preached his gospel around the world, and he was invited to address a conference on global warming at the United Nations. By 2007, a national survey found that Americans considered him a better spokesman for the environment than former Vice President Al Gore, who had been talking about little else for a decade.[2] And yet Schwarzenegger managed to burnish his green credentials while retaining the support of Republican voters and, generally, maintaining his alliance with the business community.

Although his enthusiasm for the environment seems to have come from nowhere, Schwarzenegger maintains that he always had a layman's appreciation for nature, from his outings as a boy in the Austrian countryside to his life near the Pacific Ocean as a resident of Los Angeles. But like most people, he rarely thought about the environment as a policy issue—until he decided to enter organized politics. Days after declaring that he would enter the race, Schwarzenegger flew to New York for a long-scheduled event with his after-school foundation. Bonnie Reiss, who was then his guide on environmental issues, went with him, and brought along the texts of a half-dozen speeches Teddy Roosevelt had given on the topic. On the same trip, the pair met with Robert F. Kennedy, Jr.— Maria Shriver's cousin, son of the late senator, and a crusading lawyer for environmental regulation. Kennedy suggested that Schwarzenegger consult Terry Tamminen, head of a group called the Santa Monica Baykeepers. Reiss also knew Tamminen and liked him, and she called him to ask for help.

The two men developed an instant rapport. In Schwarzenegger, Tamminen says, he found a curious vessel whose vision—protect the environment while growing the economy—just needed to be filled in with policy details. In Tamminen, Schwarzenegger says, he found a guru who could explain complicated issues in simple terms.

"I met Terry and fell in love with him," Schwarzenegger said. "It was literally like a gift from God. And he helped me . . . I remember talking to him every day for an hour or two, sometimes about the environment, about the different issues, different ideas. And slowly we started putting something together."[3]

Tamminen was a quirky, independent-minded innovator with a story that made him a natural fit for Schwarzenegger, who relishes people who, like himself, stand out in a crowd. A former sheep rancher and real estate executive who became a pool maintenance man and then wrote *The Ultimate Pool Maintenance Manual*, Tamminen speaks German, Dutch, and Spanish as well as English. He is an avid pilot of airplanes and helicopters, a licensed ship captain, and an expert on the works of William Shakespeare. He was the founder of the Santa Monica Baykeeper foundation, which works to protect the waters off the Los Angeles coast, and the director of Environment Now.

"Arnold comes from a very sincere place about the environment, but it wasn't his life," Tamminen said. "He knew what he wanted to do but he wasn't familiar with all the policies and the details of how he would do it."[4]

The two met for lunch in Schwarzenegger's Santa Monica offices with Reiss the Monday after Schwarzenegger entered the race. They talked about the environment while the candidate's children, out of school for the summer, buzzed in and out and munched on pizza. They met again several more times that week.

"We'd go through each of the topics," Tamminen said. "I'd lay things out for him, and he'd try things on for size."

Tamminen, who was not registered in a political party, said Schwarzenegger's Republican advisers "freaked out" as they began to see the environmental platform taking shape. They said it was too specific. Too ambitious. They considered Tamminen "some wacky tree hugger," he said. In the end, though, it might have been Tamminen and his wacky ideas that most defined Schwarzenegger's distinct take on governing California.

Their meetings produced a document that Schwarzenegger called his "Environmental Action Plan." The plan was packed with goals that would have been audacious for any politician, let alone a Republican. Schwarzenegger pledged to cut air pollution statewide by 50 percent, ensure that half of new homes had solar power by 2005, and require that 20 percent of the state's power needs were met by renewable fuels by 2010, seven years earlier than the standard set by his predecessor, Gray Davis. By 2020, he said, he wanted a third of the state's energy to come from renewable sources. He promised to invest in a "hydrogen highway" with filling stations for fuel cell cars every 20 miles and to get the state's worst-polluting vehicles off the road, noting that 10 percent of the cars produce half the smog that comes from mobile sources. He said he would protect the state's coastline by fighting offshore oil drilling and enforcing the Clean Water Act for local governments dumping treated sewage into the ocean. And he pledged to create a new state agency with the sole job of protecting California's majestic Sierra range. One topic, curiously enough, he hardly mentioned: global warming.

The plan, for all its ambition, said nothing about the practical policy and regulatory questions that come up all the time for the chief executive of California. And Schwarzenegger faced one of those within days after taking office. A Republican from Missouri—Christopher Bond—was trying to attach an amendment to a spending bill in the U.S. Senate that would have prohibited California from regulating pollution from engines smaller than 50 horsepower. Bond was pushing the amendment at the behest of Briggs and Stratton, a Wisconsin-based manufacturer of lawnmower engines that had two plants in Missouri. Had it passed, it would have preempted a California regulation that promised to eliminate pollution from lawnmowers, leaf blowers, and other small engines, a move equivalent to taking two million cars off the road. Operating a gas-powered lawnmower for an hour, California officials said, spewed as much air pollution as driving a car for 13 hours. California Senator Dianne Feinstein was fighting to block Bond's amendment and asked Schwarzenegger to help. The new governor did not hesitate to provide that help, calling key Republicans in Congress. Tamminen, meanwhile, recruited a surprising ally: the Western States Petroleum Association. He called the association's president and told him that if California couldn't regulate pollution from small, inefficient engines, the state would have to get even tougher on the state's oil refineries. With the help of Schwarzenegger and the oil industry, Bond's amendment was defeated and the California regulation moved forward.[5]

But as Schwarzenegger's time in office grew from days to months and years, the record on environmental issues that emerged from his actions was mixed. He was far more in favor of government intervention than most Republicans, often to the consternation of Republican activists and legislators. But he never completely abandoned his belief that markets and economic incentives could accomplish the goals of the environmental movement more efficiently and at less cost than the kind of command-and-control regulation favored by most Democrats. And even as he became a worldwide symbol of environmentalism, he insisted that no one needed to change their lifestyle in order to help save the planet. New technology, he claimed, could let us have it all: a cleaner environment, more jobs, fast cars, and private jets. His optimism was refreshing. But he also was guilty of sugar-coating the truth for his constituents, who, at least in the short term, would certainly be paying more for fuel, electricity, and consumer products thanks to the policies he advocated.

At any rate, his activism, for a Republican governor at least, was extraordinary. One of his biggest passions turned out to be the coast, which he enjoyed as a private citizen and which, in many ways, defined California in the international consciousness. He laid out a coastal protection plan and then implemented it vigorously. Through the California Fish and Game Commission, his administration enacted a major expansion of coastal reserves that limited and in some cases banned fishing in 29 marine protected areas covering more than 200 square miles along the central California coast. The Ocean Conservancy hailed the action as the historic equivalent of Teddy Roosevelt's creation of the National Park System. The idea was to protect the places fishes need to feed and breed so that they could repopulate their stocks and migrate out to areas where they could be harvested.

Schwarzenegger also signed the California Ocean Protection Act, which created a council of state agency leaders to coordinate actions against pollution, overfishing, and habitat damage. The act created an Ocean Protection trust fund to pay for conservation projects, including pollution control, research, monitoring, and enforcement. He signed legislation to ban the dumping of sewage, whether treated or not, from cruise ships in state waters, and another that banned the release of "gray water" from the ships' kitchens, laundries, and showers.

Then he turned to the state's majestic mountain range, creating the Sierra Nevada Conservancy, a new state agency designed to protect the environment and the economy of the 25-million-acre region. Like many of the environmental bills Schwarzenegger signed, the Sierra law was a compromise. And unlike a similar conservancy that had long protected the Santa Monica Mountains near his Southern California home, the Sierra Conservancy had no power to buy land, a gesture intended to win the support of local governments and others in the conservative region who were wary of moves to expand public ownership of property.

The governor also followed through on his pledge to push for alternative sources of energy. He got a lot of attention for his proposed "hydrogen highway" and for converting one of his Hummers so that it could run on the nonpolluting fuel, even though most experts considered the technology years if not decades away from being a safe, reliable, and efficient alternative to petroleum. But, typically, his more significant work was behind the scenes. He persuaded the Public Utilities Commission to adopt a new fuel standard for the state's utilities, requiring them to use renewable energy for 20 percent of their electricity generation by 2010. And, as promised, he advanced a dramatic expansion of solar power, using state conservation grant money to subsidize what he said would be one million new solar roofs, again using the utilities commission to implement his policy after Democrats in the Legislature tried to kill it to satisfy labor union concerns over who would install the solar panels. He did not, however, fulfill his pledge to enact either legislation or regulations requiring that half the new homes built in the state be equipped with solar power.

Schwarzenegger set the state on course to reduce energy usage in government buildings 20 percent by 2015 and to encourage the private sector to do the same. The state, under a "Green Buildings" executive order Schwarzenegger issued in December 2004, would adhere to national green building standards on all new buildings and on renovations larger than 10,000 square feet. Buildings of at least 50,000 square feet, meanwhile, would be renovated for energy efficiency by 2015. For every new building, the state would also evaluate the potential for clean, on-site power generation, and managers of existing state buildings were directed to take advantage of incentives designed to reduce peak-power usage.[6]

Under Tamminen's leadership, California's Environmental Protection Agency launched an aggressive enforcement initiative to improve compliance with the state's environmental laws. An initial assessment found that the state was focused on mandated inspections of people who held permits to discharge waste, while all but ignoring potential fraud and the actions of parties who never bothered to seek a permit even though they were required to do so. The status quo, the review found, was piecemeal and ineffective enforcement that was increasingly a pain for people who were honest players in the system and that let the truly bad actors off the hook. Finally, the review found that the state measured the success of its efforts by the number of inspections conducted and fines levied rather than by any measure of the level of compliance with the law.

The new effort added enforcement staff and money, used stings to trap illegal dumpers and others committing environmental crimes, and focused on areas near the Mexican border that had been virtually unwatched in the past.

All of that, however, was simply a prelude to the issue that vaulted Schwarzenegger and his environmental policies onto the national stage: global warming. Although Democrats and environmentalists have sometimes portrayed Schwarzenegger as a latecomer to the party, he was actually a leader in calling for the kind of comprehensive, statewide approach that eventually became the basis for Assembly Bill 32, the state's landmark law designed to limit greenhouse gas emissions. In June 2005, in the midst of his "Year of Reform" that was seen as a hard shift to the ideological right, Schwarzenegger veered left on the environment, issuing an executive order that called for the state to limit the emission of carbon dioxide and other greenhouse gases to 1990 levels by 2020, a reduction of 25 percent from projected levels. That order set in motion a Climate Action Team to study the problem and recommend specific solutions. Schwarzenegger signed it at a United Nations event in San Francisco, citing the threat global warming posed to California and the opportunity that the development of new, clean-fuels technology offered to the state's economy.

"As of today, California is going to be the leader in the fight against global warming," Schwarzenegger declared. "The debate is over. We know the science, we see the threat, and the time for action is now." At the time, environmentalists were thrilled, in part because Schwarzenegger, as such a visible Republican, stood in contrast to President Bush, whose administration had downplayed the threat from global warming and had rejected the idea of forcing polluters to deal with it.

"The governor is a real-life climate action hero today," gushed Nancy Ryan, a senior economist with the group Environmental Defense.[7]

But if the debate over the causes and consequences of global warming was over in Sacramento, the fight over what California could do about it was only beginning. Two months after the governor issued his executive order, Assemblywoman Fran Pavley—who had authored an earlier law requiring the automobile industry to reduce greenhouse gas emissions from the cars they sell in California—amended Assembly Bill 32 to place into the law the kind of broad attack on the problem Schwarzenegger laid out in his plan, which lacked any enforcement mechanism. Throughout the following year, Schwarzenegger and the Democrats in the Legislature would tangle over the details of that bill, which took on a higher profile when the leader of the Assembly, Speaker Fabian Núñez, signed on as a coauthor.

Schwarzenegger believed in the cause. But he also dearly wanted, and needed, the legislation as a key part of his drive to rehabilitate his image during his 2006 reelection year. Knowing this, the Democrats, led by Núñez and Senator Don Perata, pushed him as far as he was willing to go, and then some. The issues came down to who would enforce the goals, how much flexibility business would be given to comply, and whether the governor would be able to stop the process by declaring an economic emergency.

Schwarzenegger wanted implementation of the bill to be held as closely as possible to the governor's office, where he and future chief executives could most easily control it. But the Democrats, fearing that Schwarzenegger or a future governor, under pressure from big business, would use the bureaucracy to squelch the law, insisted that the job be given to the California Air Resources Board. The board's members are appointed by the governor but are required to hold public hearings and are generally more open and accessible to environmental advocates. The Democrats won on that issue.

The governor insisted, however, on having the power to pull the plug on the goals if their implementation was causing huge problems for business. Lawmakers feared this would allow the governor to gut the new rules. But mindful of the disaster that ensued after the Legislature voted to restructure the state's electricity industry in the 1990s, lawmakers agreed to give the governor the power to adjust the law's deadlines under "extraordinary circumstances, catastrophic events, or significant economic harm"—and then only for one year at a time. Schwarzenegger prevailed on that issue.

Finally, Schwarzenegger, building on a concept that had been popular in environmental circles for years, demanded that the law be implemented using a "cap and trade" system. Such a system would place a mandated limit on greenhouse gases, and then allow businesses that could not meet that limit to buy credits—the right to pollute—from other businesses that could more cheaply reduce their emissions. This kind of market system had been used with success to fight acid rain in the Northeast, but a poorly designed version had been a flop when it was tried for greenhouse gases in Europe. Well executed, a market for emission credits would be the best way to reduce greenhouse gases in the most efficient way possible. But to many Democrats, it smacked of letting big polluters off the hook. Rather than a market-based system, they wanted the law to rely mainly—or at least first—on top-down regulations requiring utilities, factories, and other industrial polluters not only to meet specific targets, but also to change industrial practices found by the state to be unacceptable.

Days before the end of the legislative session, the two sides were at a stalemate on the issue. The fate of the bill hung in the balance in a confrontation over two words: "shall" and "may." Schwarzenegger insisted that the bill require a trading system. The law, he argued, should say that the state "shall" adopt such a program as part of implementing the new greenhouse gas standards. Democrats refused to budge. They wanted to make emissions trading optional by saying that the Air Board "may" use a market-based system if it were warranted, and only after meeting certain conditions. In the end, Schwarzenegger backed down, agreeing to the language submitted by the Democrats. As long as he was reelected, he reasoned, his appointees would be in control of the Air Resources Board and he could direct them to develop the kind of cap-and-trade system he envisioned. And that is just what he did, accelerating the development of the market rules beyond what the Democrats believed the law allowed.

Schwarzenegger signed the bill—the California Global Warming Solutions Act of 2006—at an elaborate ceremony on Treasure Island in the middle of San Francisco Bay. Mayor Gavin Newsom, a Democrat, introduced him. New York Governor George Pataki was among the guests of honor. British Prime Minister Tony Blair participated via a live satellite hookup from London, his image beamed onto a massive television screen at the site. And just in case the event did not get enough attention, the entire show was repeated a few hours later in Los Angeles, even though the bill had already been signed into law.

It was still an election year, however, and some of the love that environmentalists showered on Schwarzenegger when he issued his executive order had disappeared by the time he signed a bill that essentially placed that order into law. Tom Adams, the president of the California League of Conservation Voters, called Schwarzenegger's signing of the bill an "election year ploy" to establish his environmental credentials before facing the voters again. "The Governor is attempting to mask his overall weak environmental record and the fact that he attempted to weaken this bill in the Legislature at the behest of his large corporate contributors," Adams said. "There would be no bill requiring greenhouse gas reductions to sign today if Democratic legislative leaders had not stood firm and pushed this legislation to the Governor's desk, intact."[8]

That might have been an overstatement in the heat of a partisan election battle, but Adams's comments did accurately reflect the bitterness among many environmentalists at Schwarzenegger's ability to reap international attention on the issue after compiling a record that was a different shade of green than they were used to. The California League of Conservation Voters rated him as "mediocre" in 2006, when he signed exactly 50 percent of the bills it was tracking that landed on his desk. That was a lower score than he received in either 2004 or 2005, when they rated him at 58 percent. He rejected a bill to levy a fee on every shipping container passing through the ports of Los Angeles and Long Beach to pay for programs to improve air quality, and another measure that would have required half the new cars sold in California by 2020 to use alternative fuels, while requiring service stations to offer the fuels. Another bill Schwarzenegger vetoed would have allowed the state's attorney general to recover litigation costs when it successfully prosecuted environmental cases.

The ports bill rejection was especially telling. Schwarzenegger had promised to reduce the state's reliance on debt and had said he supported the concept of "polluter pays"—folding the cost of cleaning up pollution into the products we all buy and use. One of the major goals in his Environmental Action Plan was to reduce air pollution by 50 percent. But he opposed the proposed $30 shipping container fee by labeling it a tax increase and instead touted his transportation bond measure, which would allocate $1 billion in borrowed money to projects intended to speed the transport of goods from the ports and thus reduce air pollution caused by idling trucks. A year later, Schwarzenegger said he would support the new fee—but only on his terms, which he promised to spell out in detail in 2008.

It was not just his record on legislation that defined Schwarzenegger as a centrist on the environment. There were countless other instances in which, despite his image, he moved to protect business from the impulses of the environmental community. His 2004 proposal to overhaul state government was a vivid example. The California Performance Review—the official name of his plan to "blow up the boxes" on the state's organization chart—called for collapsing the Air Resources Board, the Water Resources Control Board, and regional water quality boards into a new state Department of the Environment. That move would have centralized environmental decision making in the state bureaucracy, away from the public spotlight and public input. The change would have almost certainly favored industry lobbyists who worked full time cultivating relationships in and around the Capitol, while reducing access to decision makers from environmental groups, researchers, and local activists. Schwarzenegger withdrew the plan in the face of widespread opposition.

The governor also sided with his business allies in supporting Proposition 64 on the November 2004 ballot, a measure touted as a protection against "frivolous" lawsuits but strongly opposed by environmentalists. The proposal sought to amend the state's unfair business competition laws by allowing private lawsuits only in cases where the person suing suffered actual financial or property loss. That would effectively end the practice of private parties suing polluters on behalf of the public, a tactic that had been used to hold oil companies, foresters, and other major corporations accountable to the state's environmental laws. The measure passed by a wide margin.

Schwarzenegger never fulfilled his promise to pursue smart growth policies to limit urban sprawl. A multi-agency task force labored for months on a plan, but it ultimately produced nothing. His first transportation bond proposal had hardly any money in it for transit, and, in 2007, he pushed to shift a tax windfall away from public transit and into other programs. He also tried to eliminate the state's reimbursement to counties for property tax they lost when farmers agreed to not develop their land for a decade or more.

Schwarzenegger's appointments, while eclectic and often surprising, also demonstrated that he was not a typical environmentalist. He named a Pacific Lumber Co. lobbyist as deputy director of Cal-EPA. He put a controversial former Department of Forestry employee on the Board of Forestry, and when the Senate rejected her, he replaced her with the vice-chairman of the California Republican Party, who was an adviser to conservative Grover Norquist's Americans for Tax Reform. At the same time, he dropped two people from the board who were seen as moderate consensus builders, including the only board member who was a scientist with an advanced degree. To the state Fish and Game Commission he appointed two people considered hostile to the environment, and, in September 2005, he fired all seven members of the state Reclamation Board, which was under fire from developers for insisting too strongly on flood protection preceding the construction of new housing. In place of the academics and local government officials who had been on the board, he named three engineers, three farmers, and a lawyer for the California Farm Bureau. Only one had experience in flood control issues.

Schwarzenegger's most controversial appointment was probably naming Cindy Tuck as chairwoman of the Air Resources Board, the panel that regulates air pollution in California and that would later take on the job of fighting global warming. Tuck was a lobby-ist for the innocuous-sounding Coalition for Environmental and Economic Balance, a group that was widely seen as a front for big business and industry. In that job she had opposed new clean air rules for California power plants and the state's first global warming law, passed in 2003, which required automakers to reduce the greenhouse emissions from the cars they sold in the state. A letter from seven major environmental groups, including the Sierra Club, the League of Conservation Voters, and the Natural Resources Defense Council, said Tuck had "consistently demonstrated her willingness and ability to side with industrial polluters even when that conflicts with public health goals."[9] The Senate refused to confirm her appointment.

Schwarzenegger's reelection was opposed by the Sierra Club, the League of Conservation Voters, many other environmental groups, and most of the state's best known environmental activists. But a *Los Angeles Times* poll found that voters, by a 45 percent to 34 percent margin, trusted him more than his Democratic opponent on environmental issues. Even 21 percent of Democrats sided with Schwarzenegger on the issue.

Despite his uneven record, Schwarzenegger emerged from the election more determined than ever to make the environment a huge part of his legacy as governor. He proposed the world's first low-carbon standard that would require sellers of fuel in California to reduce the carbon content of their fuel by 10 percent by 2020, an idea that quickly gained traction in Congress and among presidential candidates from both parties. And he began a global victory lap, meeting in his office and on the road with officials from Canada, Australia, Great Britain, and elsewhere to preach his gospel on greenhouse gases.

After appearing on the covers of *Newsweek* and *Outside Magazine* in the same week, Schwarzenegger gave a major speech in Washington at which he pledged to make environmentalism "sexy" and hip, and to strip it of its image, which in his view, was built around a public guilt trip. He recalled his effect on bodybuilding, which, he said, was a strange, fringe sport that he helped turn into a mainstream activity. He would do the same, he said, for the environmental movement.

He flaunted his Hummers (since converted to run on hydrogen and biofuels) and said soccer moms wanted and should be able to have sport utility vehicles. We could drive anything we want, he said, as long as what we drive was made more fuel efficient and less polluting. That same month he taped a segment for MTV's show *Pimp My Ride*, in which he helped convert a Chevy Impala into a bio-fueled racer with an 800 horsepower engine that could go from 0 to 60 miles per hour in three seconds.

The environmental movement, Schwarzenegger said in Washington, "is about to switch over from being powered by guilt to being powered by something much more positive, much more dynamic, something much more capable of bringing about major change. . . . It is too bad, of course, that we can't all live simple lives like the Buddhist monks in Tibet. But you know something? That's not going to happen.

"I don't think that any movement has ever made it and has ever made much progress based on guilt. Guilt is passive, guilt is inhibiting, and guilt is defensive. . . . Successful movements are built on passion, they're not built on guilt. They're built on passion, they're built on confidence, and they're built on critical mass. And often, they're built on an element of alarm that galvanizes action."

Many professional environmentalists would not like his characterization of their movement or the balance he tried to strike. But Schwarzenegger's message had broad appeal. People who wanted the environment protected could get excited about the sweeping goals he laid out for government and industry. Those who were more concerned about individual freedom could be reassured by his endorsement of personal choice. Even some businesses embraced his program, especially those who were well positioned to invest in the new technologies that he was advocating.

At least until his policies moved from the abstract world of the law books to the practical reality of changing lives and bottom lines, Schwarzenegger was able to ride his green wave to acclaim around the world and political popularity at home.

TEN

The Rise of the Independent Voter

Schwarzenegger's three careers have all followed a similar path. In each case, he jumped into something that wiser men might have considered folly. Then he spotted a trend, caught it, added his own special imprint, and rode it to international fame.

As a young man, he sculpted his body and then changed body-building itself from a fringe sport into a mainstream passion. Next he took his pumped-up physique, heavy Austrian accent, and marginal acting skills to Hollywood, where he helped vitalize the action movie genre, employing special effects and gratuitous violence to create films that won loyal audiences around the world. And now, having been elected governor of California without a day of elected political experience, he has tapped into the rise of the independent voter in a time of widespread disgust with America's two major political parties. He is still trying to make that wave his own and ride it to revolutionary change in our political system.

If Schwarzenegger hadn't jumped into politics when he did, someone might have had to invent him. He is the ideal politician for this independent, Internet-driven age, for an electorate with little patience for policy details or petty partisanship but a thirst for problem-solving, results-oriented politics. His visions are sweeping, his projects huge. His ideology hopscotches across the political battlefield, plucking positions from right, left, and center, sometimes melding all three. He wants results, and though he does not always get them, his obvious yearning to move forward, try new things, and take risks endears him to a new kind of voter who wants government to work for a change.

"People are more interested in getting things done," Schwarzenegger said. "They just want to get the roads built, they want to get a better education system, they want to have better health care, less expensive health care. They just want to get things done."[1]

Or, as he said in his second inaugural address:

"We don't need Republican roads or Democratic roads. We need roads. We don't need Republican health care or Democratic health care. We need health care.

"We don't need Republican clean air or Democratic clean air. We all breathe the same air."

It's not that simple, of course. There are different ways to build roads, provide health care, and clean the air, and people of different beliefs are going to disagree on how to go about it. The dividing line is typically the extent to which government will be involved, and spend money, in seeking to reach those goals. And Schwarzenegger sometimes demonizes those he accuses of "partisanship" in much the same way that the partisans tend to demonize each other.

But his greater point is that there is nothing sacred in anyone's approach to the issues that concern Californians and people everywhere. And there is nothing wrong with meeting your opposition half way to get the traffic moving or broaden access to health care or reduce air pollution. That is a message that sends chills up the spines of principled partisans but resonates with independent voters, who, unlike the true believers on the edge of the two major parties, value problem solving more than ideology.

Even before Schwarzenegger came along, California's voter rolls were shedding Democrats and Republicans while gaining independents, people who choose "decline to state" when they register to vote and who are asked which party they want to join. Now that trend is accelerating, and it may be an early indicator of where the rest of the nation will soon be headed.

Between the time Schwarzenegger was first elected in 2003 and the time he was inaugurated for his second term a little more than three years later, California added a net of about a quarter-million voters to its rolls. But during that same 40-month period, both major parties actually lost registration. The Democrats lost about 68,000 voters. The Republican Party's numbers fell by 86,000. Most of the minor parties lost voters as well. The ranks of voters who chose no party, meanwhile, swelled by 450,000. And that was only the continuation of a trend that has been going on for more than a decade. California, like much of the nation, appears headed toward a politics based more on individual candidates than on party preference. Already, 23 percent of the state's electorate falls outside the two major parties. The Democrats have held an edge over the Republicans in California for decades, and that margin still exists. But both parties are slipping below the tide. The latest numbers showed the Democrats with just 42.5 percent of the vote and the Republicans with 34 percent. If current trends continue, within a generation, voters who belong to neither party will be a plurality in the state.

"The Democratic Party and the Republican Party are still going to be around, but they are going to have little more influence than the League of Women Voters and the Sierra Club," said David Lesher, government affairs director for the Public Policy Institute of California, which has done extensive research on the phenomenon. "The parties will be a measure of where these candidates are coming from and will tell you something about them. But the way campaigns will be run, the way voters decide, will be done in much more of an open market."[2]

The trend has coincided with the onset of the information age and seems connected to it. The Internet is helping to break up large institutions that have dominated society for generations. This has been most profound in the world of commerce, where small companies become big overnight and big companies lose their grip on the consumer. Young adults today grew up shopping online for books (if they read), music (if they pay for it), clothes, and electronics. They buy their airline tickets, book hotels, and rent cars at a discount on the Internet, grab bargains off eBay; and rent apartments that they find on Craigslist. They pay their bills and manage their investments on the computer. They barely even use e-mail anymore, having replaced that transitional form of contact with text messages. They arrange their own music selections on iPods. They create their own television schedule using digital video recorders. And if they follow public affairs, it almost certainly is not through the print version of the local newspaper or the nightly network news. It is on the Internet, perhaps through an established mainstream media site, but just as likely through blogs, aggregators, or chat rooms.

That same wave of decentralization is sweeping politics. New voters, and many older ones, are less inclined to take the word of the major parties. They want to think for themselves and make their own decisions, even if that means crossing party lines and ignoring traditional philosophical constraints.

"We are entering a post-ideological world," says Jim Mangia, the former national secretary for Ross Perot's Reform Party who now helps run a group called IndependentVoice.org that is attempting to help independents network with one another in hopes of shifting the political debate.

Roger L. Simon, a screenwriter and author who started his own blog and then expanded it into Pajamas Media, a network of independent citizen journalists, calls ideology a "nineteenth century" approach to life. "Ideology is a form of intellectual blinders," says Simon, a liberal Democrat whose vote for Schwarzenegger in 2003 was the first he ever cast for a Republican. "It gives you an excuse not to think." Simon used to vote a party line, and in nonpartisan local races where he knew little about the candidate, he would usually rely on the endorsements in his local alternative weekly. But now, he says, information is so widely available that he can quickly size up the candidates on his own—and make his own decisions.

Independent voters are more likely to be male, younger, and college educated than voters who belong to one of the two major parties, according to research by the Public Policy Institute of California. As a group, they are more ethnically diverse than the Republicans, but not as diverse as the Democrats, except that Asians make up twice as big a share of independents as they do Democrats. Not surprisingly, independents are also more likely than the voters of either party to describe themselves as "middle of the road" rather than liberal or conservative. Forty-two percent use that term to describe themselves, compared with 33 percent of Democrats and just 27 percent of Republicans.

In a national poll focusing on independents for the *Washington Post*, the Kaiser Family Foundation, and Harvard University, 36 percent of voters identified themselves as Democrats, 27 percent as Republicans, and 29 percent as independents. Although the number of true independents was up only slightly from the 27 percent who described themselves as independent to exit pollsters in the November 2006 elections, only 19 percent of those surveyed for the *Post* said they were "strong Democrats" and 16 percent said they were "strong Republicans." By far the biggest group was made up of independents and those who were registered to one party or the other but were not wedded to their choice.

Despite what appears to be a growing number of independents, however, many academics and political consultants insist that the rise of the independent voter is overblown. Most of those voters, these experts contend, are actually aligned with one major party or the other. It's just that they either don't know it, or they don't care for others to know it.

In *The Myth of the Independent Voter*, Raymond Wolfinger, a UC Berkeley political scientist, and his coauthors used polls from presidential elections from 1952 to 1988 to conclude that most people who describe themselves as independents behave like either Republicans or Democrats when they go to the polls.[3]

One problem with that analysis, though, is that the polling data on which it was based measured opinion and behavior only in narrowly partisan elections. By their nature, these contests force independents to choose one side or another in a highly charged environment. When independent voters have more choices, either among the candidates or on issues, they do swing from side to side on the ideological spectrum. California's experience proves that.

In the 2006 election, for example, 53 percent of independents voted for Schwarzenegger. But only 39 percent voted for his more conservative running mate, Republican state Senator Tom McClintock. And fewer still, 29 percent, voted for another Republican senator, Charles Poochigian, in the race for attorney general against former governor Jerry Brown. And while a majority of independents were voting for Schwarzenegger, a majority also chose Democratic U.S. Senator Dianne Feinstein, sending her to a third full term in Congress.

How can the same voters split their tickets so wildly? One reason is that independents, when viewed as a group, are hybrids, pulling positions from both parties. Like Democrats, the majority of independents tend to be social liberals or almost libertarian on certain issues, supporting abortion rights, medical marijuana, physician-assisted suicide, and increased immigration. But like Republicans, most independents also oppose affirmative action, bilingual education, the expansion of government-run health care, and universal preschool. They tend to be more leery of taxes than Democrats but more open to them than Republicans. Independents also appear to be shifting on the socially explosive issue of gay marriage. A majority of them joined with Republicans in passing a ballot proposition in 2000 to ban gay marriage in California. But today, more independents support gay marriage than oppose it, and their shift may be opening the door to a change in that policy in California.

An examination of the results of recent ballot measures and exit polls of voters paints an even more vivid picture. Since 1996, there have been 42 ballot measures in California for which public exit poll data exist. On those 42 questions, independents, taken as a group, were on the losing side only 5 times, compared with 10 times for Democrats and 17 for Republicans.

Fourteen times, the independents lined up with the Democrats to pass or block a measure when the Republicans were on the other side. That included passing bond measures for water, housing, schools, and stem cell research, and defeating all four of Schwarzenegger's measures in the 2005 special election. The independents and the Democrats also united to adopt the state's medical marijuana law, defeat an attempt to restrict the use of union dues for political activity, expand Indian gaming, and block an initiative that sought to prohibit the collection of racial and ethnic data by government agencies. And they teamed up to defeat a Republican-backed measure that would have forced the losers in certain lawsuits to pay the winners' legal fees.

Eight other times, independents voted with the Republicans on the winning side of an issue. Those included successful votes to ban affirmative action, bilingual education, and gay marriage, and to defeat a measure that would have lowered the vote threshold for local school bonds to a simple majority. Independents and Republicans also teamed up to reject expansions of government-mandated health care and pre-school for all four-year-olds, and to uphold term limits. And they famously combined to recall Governor Gray Davis from office in 2003 and replace him with Schwarzenegger.

Yet it is easy to misunderstand independent voters. Every voting bloc is a statistical aggregation of individuals, not a single organism. For that reason, it is dangerous to generalize about how independents feel about this issue or that one, because any number of individual independents might think just the opposite. If 60 percent of independents voted for the bond measure to finance stem cell research, for example, that means 40 percent voted against it. And if the vote were 50–50, that does not mean that independents are centrist or wishy-washy, it just means that half of them had one opinion and half had the other. They might all be extremely passionate about their beliefs.

Another common perception about independents is that they are detached from the political process. Bill Cavala, a former long-time political aide to the Democrats in the California Assembly, says voters who refuse to choose a party are the "least interested, least informed folk who take the trouble to exercise the franchise. . . . These people pay very little attention to government or politics. They make their political decision in a context quite different than most of us. They don't pay attention to campaign activity until the choice is upon them and they must."[4]

It is true that independents vote in fewer numbers than do their counterparts who are registered in the major parties. But recent surveys suggest that independents who do vote know as much about politics and policy as do party members. Asked how closely they had followed the campaign preceding the November 2006 election, 77 percent of independents who voted said "very closely" or "fairly closely," compared with 79 percent of Republicans and 76 percent of Democrats. Independents tended to get less of their information from television advertising and the mainstream media than did members of the two major parties. Instead, they relied more on the Internet, with 13 percent saying it was their primary source of information, compared with 9 percent for Republicans and 6 percent for Democrats. And a poll in May 2007 showed that most California voters had only a loose familiarity with the state's finances, suggesting that they were making decisions without really knowing the context or the consequences of their actions. But independents were at least as well informed as the members of the major parties. Asked to name the largest single area of state government spending, 34 percent of independents correctly named kindergarten through 12th grade education, compared with 36 percent of Republicans and 29 percent of Democrats who got that question right. And slightly more independents than party members correctly identified the state's single largest source of revenue—the personal income tax. Thirty-five percent of independent voters answered that question correctly, compared with 34 percent of Republicans and 32 percent of Democrats.

Schwarzenegger's political fortunes have been tied to independents from the beginning, even before he ever ran for office. His predecessor, Gray Davis, saw his troubles begin when he lost the trust of independent voters. In 1998, Davis swept into office in a landslide while winning the independent vote over the state's conservative attorney general, Dan Lungren, by a margin of 60 percent to 28 percent, according to the *Los Angeles Times* exit poll. But four years later, running against another conservative—businessman Bill Simon, a neophyte politician whose campaign was plagued by blunders—Davis barely held the independents, winning by a margin of 39 percent to 38 percent. Even more ominous, a stunning 23 percent of independent voters chose neither Davis nor Simon, expressing their dismay at the choice presented them by voting for one of the minor-party candidates. And 7 percent of independents who went to the polls did not even bother to vote in the governor's race at all. That frustration was a leading indicator of the recall election that would sweep Davis from office a year later.

Schwarzenegger also benefited directly from his ability to run for governor in the special election that was held at the same time as the recall. While he might have been challenged to win a Republican primary dominated by conservatives, the special election was a winner-takes-all affair in which all the voters could choose among all the candidates, regardless of party. Schwarzenegger was able to appeal to voters across the spectrum with his call for balancing the budget and sweeping the "special interests" out of Sacramento while barely mentioning that he was a Republican in a state dominated by Democrats. His hybrid message—liberal on social issues, conservative on fiscal issues, and progressive on the environment—resonated with independent voters, who chose him by a margin of 46 percent to 27 percent over his closest rival, Democratic Lieutenant Governor Cruz Bustamante.[5]

Once in office, Schwarzenegger's standing rose and fell and rose again as independents warmed to him, went cold, and then came back to his camp. In August 2004, Schwarzenegger's approval ratings reached a stratospheric 69 percent among likely voters, with 24 percent disapproving of the job he was doing. Among independents, his margin was 66 percent to 26 percent. But that would soon begin to change. In September of that year, Schwarzenegger spoke before a national television audience in prime time at the Republican Convention nominating President Bush to a second term. While his speech was not overly partisan, it did include a section explaining why he was a Republican. In it, he mentioned that he was first drawn to the party after hearing Richard Nixon campaigning in 1968, hardly a story designed to draw nonpartisans into the fold. The next month, Schwarzenegger started campaigning in earnest for Republican candidates running for the Legislature, and then, the weekend before the election, he made a quick trip to Ohio to campaign for Bush. As it happened, Bush won the state narrowly, and Ohio was seen as pivotal to his national victory.

Throughout that fall and winter, Schwarzenegger's approval ratings began to drift slowly downward, and after he released a budget that cut the growth in education spending and laid out an agenda that challenged Democratic interests and allies in the Capitol, his ratings plunged. By April, Schwarzenegger's job approval rating had gone negative, with 45 percent approving and 47 percent disapproving. He still had strong support among Republicans, but only 40 percent of independents liked the job he was doing while 49 percent did not. Democrats were even more negative.

Joe Gandelman is an independent whose own experience was a perfect reflection of the polls. A San Diegan who runs a blog called "The Moderate Voice,"[6] Gandelman voted for Davis twice, then voted for the recall and Schwarzenegger.

"I am the quintessential independent," Gandelman says.[7] "I like candidates who are not super-ideological." Gandelman said his vote for Schwarzenegger in 2003 was one of the few he has cast recently that he actually "felt good" about. But then, as the governor turned to the right and grew more confrontational with Democrats, Gandelman grew uneasy. By the time of the special election in 2005, he says, he felt betrayed.

"I voted against everything he proposed in the special election," Gandelman said. He admits that some of the ideas in Schwarzenegger's initiatives appealed to him, but his votes, he said, were intended to send a message: he didn't like the governor's tactics or his rhetoric. "I didn't want to give him any support."

But just as quickly, after Schwarzenegger apologized for pushing too hard and too fast, and for making politics personal, Gandelman turned back around. He voted for Schwarzenegger again when he ran for reelection.

Gandelman had plenty of company as he swung back and forth. A poll in March 2006 found that independent voters (as well as many Democrats and Republicans) felt good about Schwarzenegger as a person even as his approval rating remained dangerously low for an incumbent seeking reelection. In the survey, 70 percent of independents said they liked Schwarzenegger, with 31 percent saying they liked him and his policies and 39 percent saying they liked him personally but did not like his policies. As his policies changed, or at least the policies he chose to promote widely, those independents returned to his side. And many Democrats soon followed.

Matthew Dowd, the chief strategist for Schwarzenegger's re-election campaign, said the governor made a deliberate attempt to appeal to independents as he ran for a second term. That strategy made sense for at least two reasons. First, since Republicans represent barely a third of California's registered voters, he needed a big chunk of the independents if he was going to win. And second, the language he would use to win over the independents would also send a signal to wavering Democrats that he would be open to their ideas.

"That's the way the governor is, the way he speaks," Dowd said. "His positions, how he talks about social issues, the compassion, tolerance, all of those sorts of things, those values, are great appeals to independents. If you look at where the people are, most of the people in this country are, they are fairly consistent on all of those things, on tolerance, on compassion, on respect for other peoples' rights. Those are like prisms on which they judge a person on all the rest of the things, the economy and all of that. But they want somebody who has those reflected values. And he does."[8]

On an Election Day when Democrats nationally took over control of the House of Representatives and the Senate for the first time in 12 years, Schwarzenegger won in California by a margin of 56 percent to 39 percent. His victory was sweeping. His margin: nearly 1.5 million votes. He won 52 of the state's 58 counties. Angelides managed to carry just four Bay Area counties (but not Santa Clara, home of the Silicon Valley, or Contra Costa, which often goes Democratic), plus Santa Cruz and Los Angeles. In the six Southern California counties outside Los Angeles—where about one-fourth of the state's voters reside, where the "Reagan Democrats" first emerged, and where the parties to this day battle over swing voters—Schwarzenegger did not just defeat Angelides, he wiped him out, by a margin of 66 percent to 30 percent.

Statewide, he won among Republicans by 91 percent to 6 percent, according to a *Los Angeles Times* exit poll. He took the independent vote by a margin of 53 percent to 34 percent. He won 26 percent of the Democratic vote. And even as he was widely seen as moving to the left, he won 84 percent of the vote from self-described conservatives and 54 percent from moderates.

The *Los Angeles Times* poll also showed how Schwarzenegger was able to reach the rising tide of independent voters. By a margin of 43 percent to 31 percent, they said Schwarzenegger would do a better job on education. On the environment, 41 percent said Schwarzenegger would do a better job, while only 29 percent said Angelides was better on that issue. On the state budget, independent voters sided with him by a margin of 52 percent to 24 percent. And on illegal immigration, the margin was 44 percent to 21 percent in Schwarzenegger's favor.

Schwarzenegger's voters most often cited his "leadership qualities" and his "clear vision for California's future" as reasons for siding with him. The top reason given by voters who chose Angelides: "He was the best of a bad lot."

Schwarzenegger's formula for his stunning comeback was not complicated. He listened to what he thought the voters had told him in 2005. He responded. And they rewarded him for it. Through an appeal to independents, he also reached Democrats while holding on to his Republican base. It was an extraordinary achievement.

But once he was reelected, a new challenge awaited him. Conservative Republican lawmakers who had tolerated his centrism to help him win a second term no longer felt any obligation to stand by him. And Democratic legislators who might have secretly wanted him to succeed in 2006 now felt more emboldened to attack him again. He was the man in the middle, which in American politics, is a lonely place to be.

PART III

UNFINISHED BUSINESS

As he began his second term, Schwarzenegger kept his Republican Party registration but proclaimed a new era of "post-partisanship," in which he said he would work across party lines to address the major issues of the day. His approach, if successful, could ultimately redefine what it means to be a Republican. But it could also change the nature of American politics itself. His notion that politics should be about governing from the center, melding the best of the left and the right, rather than winning at all costs, could not have been more alien to the culture that prevailed in Washington at the time and in many of the nation's state capitols. On a series of major issues that have divided the parties nationally and across the country, Schwarzenegger sought to form coalitions that would bridge historic differences. He supported a health-care reform that combined personal responsibility with government mandates and subsidies, immigration reform that linked better border security to the legalization of undocumented immigrants, a prison overhaul that focused on punishment and rehabilitation, and an education program that combined high standards and greater support for the children of the poor. His other big idea—changing the way political district boundaries were drawn—went to the very core of the nation's partisan political system and was aimed squarely at opening the door to the election of more politicians like him, whose views could not be neatly confined to the agendas of one major party or the other.

ELEVEN

To Your Health

One of the first things young Arnold Schwarzenegger did after arriving in America, he says, was buy health insurance. As an athlete, a bodybuilder lifting hundreds of pounds to tone his muscles, injury was always a risk, and he figured he would need insurance if he had to find medical care. Besides, he had always had insurance in Austria. Everyone had insurance there, as part of the government system. Compared to what he was used to at home, America's health insurance system seemed "primitive," he said. He was surprised that even people who could afford to buy insurance often went without it.

"I come from a country where it was so normal, that everyone had insurance," he said. "I grew up with the culture that everyone has to participate." In the United States, he found, "People felt that they don't need to have coverage, because the emergency room will accept you anyway. But . . . someone . . . has to pay for it."[1]

From the time he became governor, he said, he wanted to propose a comprehensive plan to deal with the issue. At the same time, he did not support the kind of government-run system that many Democrats favored. Nor did he want to place the bulk of the burden on employers, because he feared doing so would be a tax on hiring that would discourage companies from creating new jobs. As a candidate in 2003, he opposed legislation that sought to do just that, and after it passed and he was elected governor, he helped lead a campaign to persuade the voters to repeal it. He vetoed bills to expand access for children, he said, because those measures would have taken hundreds of millions of dollars from the treasury at a time when the government was running a deficit. Although he didn't make this clear at the time, he said later that he always wanted to develop a complete plan to cover everyone, with its own source of funding so that it would be, at least from the government's perspective, "revenue neutral."

After winning a second term in November 2006, Schwarzenegger's first move was to put the finishing touches on a plan for universal health care that he had promised the voters during the campaign. The media had not taken his pledge all that seriously, since the governor had opposed earlier efforts to expand the state's role in extending access to insurance, and he had harshly criticized his opponent, Democrat Phil Angelides, for offering a plan to require large employers to provide coverage. Schwarzenegger attacked that proposal as a massive tax increase, but behind the scenes, a bipartisan group of advisers was working feverishly to fashion an even bigger plan that Schwarzenegger could present early in 2007.

That group's task was to break through the ideological logjam that had prevented most states and the national government from addressing the issue. Democrats tended to prefer either a single-payer, Canadian-style plan or a combination of government mandates and taxes to cover everyone. Republicans focused on personal responsibility and argued that insurance had been loaded up with so many mandates already that it no longer served its original purpose: protecting people against an unexpected illness or injury so expensive that it created a financial hardship or could even drive a family into bankruptcy.

Schwarzenegger's effort was led by a liberal Democrat, Daniel Zingale, who was officially First Lady Maria Shriver's chief of staff but who also served as a senior adviser to the governor. Zingale was smart, driven, and, as a former AIDS activist and political director of the Human Rights Campaign, passionate about health care. He worked closely with Kim Belshe, the secretary of the Health and Human Services Agency, who had also been health services director for California's former Republican governor, Pete Wilson. Together they directed a team of advisers that, in typical Schwarzenegger fashion, included both big-government Democrats and Republicans sympathetic to business.

The plan they devised was an ideological hybrid. It was built on the idea of personal responsibility: everyone should have health insurance, to protect themselves, their assets, and the taxpayers.

"If you want health care, you're responsible for it," Schwarzenegger said. "Not someone else. You. You're responsible for it."[2]

In theory this was a conservative idea, and conservative think tanks had been kicking it around for years. But it is one thing to encourage personal responsibility, or even to provide incentives for people to buy insurance. It's another for the government to require them to do so, as Schwarzenegger was proposing. That is where he parted company with the economic conservatives he still liked to consider his allies—even if they considered him a dangerous turncoat.

In Schwarzenegger's plan, this "individual mandate" was paired with an idea popular on the left: strict new requirements on the insurance industry. Insurers doing business in California would be forced to provide coverage to anyone who applied, regardless of preexisting health conditions. They would also have to charge everyone in a particular plan the same premiums, except for differences to account for age and geography. And they would have to spend at least 85 percent of the premiums they collected on health care, leaving just 15 percent for administration, marketing, and profits.

These two ideas—the individual mandate and the requirement that insurers guarantee coverage to all who applied—were joined as an intellectual pair. If the state only required insurers to cover everyone regardless of their health condition, people would have little incentive to buy insurance until they were sick. It would be like allowing people to buy home insurance when their house was on fire, or letting motorists purchase automobile coverage after an accident. While many healthy people might buy coverage anyway, out of habit or an extra measure of caution, the insurance pool would eventually be weighted toward the sick and the injured, and the cost of coverage would rise, as it had in those states that adopted such a policy. The individual mandate, Schwarzenegger argued, worked in the other direction by expanding the insurance pool to include everyone, even young, healthy people who were most likely to avoid covering themselves until they had a problem.

Once Schwarzenegger and his team decided that everyone would have to have insurance, they had to decide how people were going to obtain that coverage. Again, the plan chose a hybrid approach, with the financial responsibility split among employers, individuals, health care providers, and the government. Employers of 10 or more people would be required to spend at least 4 percent of their payroll on health care or else pay a fee to the state, which would use the money to buy insurance for people who did not have coverage. People earning more than two and a half times the federal poverty level, or about $50,000 for a family of four, would have to pay premiums to cover whatever portion was not paid by their employer. The poorest of the poor would continue to get coverage through Medi-Cal, the state's program for the needy, and the working poor would get subsides from the state and pay between 3 percent and 6 percent of their income for coverage.

Anyone getting their coverage through the state would have a comprehensive package of benefits with preventive care, drug coverage, and low deductibles and co-payments. Those buying coverage on their own would be allowed to satisfy the mandate, if they chose to do so, by buying low-cost plans designed mainly to protect them from financial disaster in the event of a major illness. With a $5,000 deductible, that kind of coverage would still leave consumers paying for most of their routine medical bills themselves. But if they were hit with costs that ran into the tens of thousands of dollars, they would be insulated from the ruin that those kinds of bills can cause.

In addition to the fee charged to employers who did not provide coverage to their workers, Schwarzenegger proposed a 2 percent tax on doctors' revenues, and a 4 percent tax on hospitals. It seemed odd to be charging the providers of health care to help defray the cost of that care. But there was a rationale behind it: the charges on doctors and hospitals would be used to pay for expanding coverage for the poor, which would then attract matching funds from the federal government. Even after paying the taxes, Schwarzenegger argued, many hospitals and doctors would come out ahead in the deal because they would no longer be stuck with the cost of paying for the uninsured, and they would be getting a big increase in reimbursements from the state for caring for the poor. Altogether, the plan was estimated to cost about $12 billion. But with the federal government kicking in more than $5 billion and individuals newly eligible for more than $8 billion in tax breaks, Californians, Schwarzenegger claimed, would do better than break even in the end.

"It's not really a tax, because in the end they're all going to benefit, and they're going to make more money because of it, because hospitals are not going to have all the uninsured people there," he said.[3]

Schwarzenegger's plan combined his own belief that everyone should have coverage, his belief in personal responsibility, and his still-lingering suspicion of government. Like him, it had internal contradictions. It was ideologically diverse. And to demonstrate that diversity, Schwarzenegger's aides did something unusual. Rather than roll out the plan with a press conference packed with supporters, they pulled together a panel of experts to discuss the plan on the day he unveiled it. None of the panelists endorsed the plan in advance, and some would prove to be quite hostile to its provisions. Even during the session convened by the governor, there were complaints: about the mandates on employers and individuals, and about the taxes. Schwarzenegger, for his part, said he was not wedded to any of the details.

The early reaction from voters was overwhelmingly positive. One independent poll found that 71 percent of California adults said they would favor a plan that required everyone to have insurance, with the cost "shared by employers, health care providers and individuals." That concept was supported by 79 percent of Democrats and 70 percent of independents. Even among Republicans, it was favored by a margin of 52 percent to 42 percent. On the idea of an employer mandate, 75 percent said companies should be required to provide insurance to their workers. Republicans supported this notion by a margin of 56 percent to 40 percent.

But the reception in the Capitol was not nearly as warm. Republican lawmakers opposed the taxes, the new insurance regulations, and a provision to cover children even if they were illegal immigrants. Many accused Schwarzenegger of selling out the principles he had just defended in his campaign for a second term.

"Phil Angelides said he would raise taxes for a health care plan, and Arnold Schwarzenegger ruthlessly attacked Angelides for that proposal and made it the centerpiece of his campaign," said state Senator Tom McClintock, a San Fernando Valley Republican and the state's leading fiscal conservative. "Now, Arnold Schwarzenegger is doing the same thing. As much as I disagreed with Phil Angelides, at least he was honest about what he intended to do."[4]

Neither McClintock nor any other elected Republican bought Schwarzenegger's reasoning that his proposal would wipe out a "hidden tax" of $14 billion—more than his program's price tag—

that was the cost of paying for the uninsured. Or that bringing in billions more in federal money and tax breaks than he was asking Californians to contribute meant that he wasn't raising taxes at all. Some mocked his description of "post-partisanship," saying the governor's new style represented a capitulation to the opposition Democrats. But if that were the case, someone forgot to tell the Democrats. They saw the governor's plan as, well, too conservative.

State Senator Sheila Kuehl, chairwoman of the Senate Health Committee and an advocate for a single-payer system, said Schwarzenegger's plan amounted to "mandatory substandard" insurance. "Universal health care doesn't mean some, it doesn't mean most, it certainly doesn't mean some of the time. It does not mean you've got to buy it whether you can afford it or not," Kuehl said at a rally outside the Capitol. "That is not universal health care."[5]

Other Democrats were not as blunt, but they were hardly more enthusiastic. The leaders of the state Legislature—Assembly Speaker Fabian Núñez and Senate Leader Don Perata—introduced plans of their own that in some ways were more modest than Schwarzenegger's. They later merged their plans into one that covered fewer people, relied on a narrower tax base, did not expand public care as much, and tinkered less with the private insurance market than did the governor's proposal.

The Democrats' plan proposed an employer mandate and taxes to extend coverage to all working Californians. An economic analysis commissioned by the leaders concluded that the proposal could be financed by a 7.5 percent payroll tax on employers who did not spend at least that much on health care for their employees. Low-income workers would be subsidized, and no one would have to pay more than 5 percent of his or her income for health care. The self-employed, and retired people not yet old enough to qualify for Medicare, were not covered by the Democrats' plan.

Republican lawmakers found themselves, once again, on the edges of the discussion. There was disagreement about whether either Schwarzenegger's plan or the Democrats' proposals could become law without a two-thirds vote in the Legislature. If the charges were to be considered fees, a majority vote would suffice. If they were considered taxes, the California Constitution required a supermajority for passage—and the cooperation of at least a handful of Republicans, which seemed unlikely. Schwarzenegger said repeatedly that he was trying to get Republicans on board, but all but one of them had signed a pledge refusing to vote for new taxes of any kind.

Instead, Republicans proposed using existing tobacco tax money to expand community clinics and health insurance for low-income children. They wanted more tax breaks to encourage individuals to buy their own coverage. And they wanted to remove some of the barriers blocking the creation of neighborhood clinics run by registered nurses or nurse practitioners under the supervision of doctors. Their plans, essentially, sought to preserve the status quo for those who had coverage while making direct care, rather than insurance, more available to low-income people who did not have coverage.

Schwarzenegger embraced those ideas and said he hoped they would be folded into whatever plan the Legislature eventually adopted. But he kept pushing for his own proposal, even as questions about its consequences mounted. To the extent that he relied on payroll contributions from employers and required workers to pay no more than a set percentage of their income, his program risked quickly running out of money. Since wages had been growing more slowly than health-care costs, and would probably continue to do so, any plan to finance health care with payroll taxes meant paying for an increasingly costly commodity with an income stream that was stagnant. Also, his proposal for a 4 percent tax on payroll for employers who did not spend at least that much on health care prompted worries that employers who were already spending more than that amount might simply dump their insurance and pay the fee instead. And no one really knew if his plan to pair an individual mandate with new requirements on the insurance industry would work, or if the market would implode under the pressure of serving so many more people with serious health conditions.

Still, the governor's plan prompted a flurry of activity and discussion, even among its opponents. While the doctors and hospitals were at first opposed to the taxes in the proposal, they worked behind the scenes to try to find a way to get more federal dollars into California without hitting their bottom lines. Eventually, the state's largest association of hospitals endorsed the proposal. And while the state's biggest insurer—Blue Cross—opposed the idea of requiring insurers to cover everyone without regard to preexisting conditions, five other insurance companies put together a plan they said could make that idea work. Business groups were generally opposed, but some individual companies that provided insurance for their workers liked the idea of requiring their competition to do the same.

Steve Burd, chairman and CEO of Safeway, Inc., the grocery store chain, built a coalition of employers that included Longs Drugs, Del Monte Foods, Bumble Bee tuna, and Pacific Gas & Electric to push for reform, with the implicit suggestion that they believed an employer mandate was acceptable. Burd, for his part, said that the 4 percent tax in the governor's plan was too low. He was also a big believer in incentives and had introduced a plan at his company that empowered employees while focusing on wellness and preventive care. The result: Safeway saved 11 percent in the first year, even as health-care inflation generally continued to soar.

"Everybody needs to be in the system," Burd said. "Think about the uninsured. They get zero preventive care, and then the care they get is at emergency, which costs about 50 percent more. And so if they were in the system, 25 percent of them would be paying, and they would stop getting emergency care, and get normal, efficient care. And if they were in a proper system where it was driven with healthy lifestyle behavior incentives, they would have a lot of prevention in the equation."[6]

The 2007 legislative session ended without Schwarzenegger's proposed health plan even coming to a vote. Despite widespread public support for the concept, the governor could not find a lawmaker in either party willing to sponsor his bill in the Legislature, and even if he had, the measure would have been voted down in its first committee hearing. But Schwarzenegger called the Legislature back into a special session to continue working on the issue, and a consensus seemed to be within reach. Democratic leaders promised to work with the governor to find common ground, the hospitals were lobbying hard for the tax on their own revenues to bring in more federal matching funds, and several business associations endorsed either the payroll tax or a sales tax in its place. But it was clear that none of those taxes were going to pass muster with the Republicans in the Legislature, and without their votes, no plan could ever get the two-thirds majority it needed for passage. So Schwarzenegger started talking to Democrats—and to Republicans outside the Legislature—about taking a plan directly to the voters.

Once again, as a Republican in the Capitol, Schwarzenegger would stand alone.

TWELVE

"I Am an Immigrant"

Schwarzenegger's life story made him the perfect politician to navigate the tricky waters of the immigration issue. But for most of his first term in office, he squandered the unique opportunity his resume presented him.

He tried to please everyone on the volatile question of giving driver's licenses to illegal immigrants, and instead angered just about everybody. He ignored the immigration issue altogether for months on end, acting as if Mexico and its millions of recent immigrants to his state barely existed. When he did return to the matter, it was to stoke the fears and frustrations that have always been present in California's Anglo population, as he briefly embraced the angriest elements of the anti-immigration movement. Later, as Congress took up the issue, he waffled, trying to sound both tough and compassionate—but endorsing nothing. It was not until the summer and fall of his reelection campaign that Schwarzenegger finally found his voice on immigration, backing a combination of measures to secure the border while supporting a guest worker program and leaving open a pathway to citizenship for those already in the country without legal papers. That seemed like a natural position for him, and it was a popular one with the voters. The wonder is that it took him so long to get there.

America is often called a nation of immigrants, but for many, that idea is abstract, a reflection more of history than contempo-

rary life. In California, however, the description applies now more
than ever. Whites are a minority in the state, representing just 44
percent of the population, and 26 percent of California's residents
were born in another country, according to the 2000 census. In that
year, nearly half the children aged five or younger had at least one
parent not born in this country. Of people five years old and older,
4 in 10 lived in a home where a language other than English was
spoken. The state's schools are packed with immigrants and the
children of immigrants, its rosters of new businesses and new
homeowners are filled with Asian and Hispanic surnames, and its
prisons house thousands of illegal immigrants convicted of serious
and violent crimes. But California no longer stands alone as an immigration magnet. As the state's housing prices soared and its job
opportunities became more scarce, immigrants started looking
elsewhere, and other states are picking up the slack. California's
share of the nation's foreign-born population peaked in 1990 at
about 33 percent, and then dropped to 28 percent 10 years later. It
will still be years before any other state challenges California's lead
as a center for immigrants, but in the year 2000, 15 states had
foreign-born populations greater than 10 percent. Among them
were Massachusetts, Connecticut, and Rhode Island. And many of
those states are going through or are about to experience some of
the same growing pains California has faced for a generation.

As an immigrant himself but also a conservative, as an embodi-
ment of the American Dream, Schwarzenegger was in the ideal position to lead a civil discussion of the issue. He could remind people
that immigration has been the engine that kept the economy growing for centuries, that it is the source of our dynamism as a nation.
He could bring attention to the positive contributions of immigrants
and argue against attempts to limit legal immigration. And he could
also say, with the sincerity of an immigrant, that he believed illegal
immigration was wrong. Not immoral. Not evil. Not a scourge of society. But wrong, because we are a nation of laws and even new-

comers need to respect them. Illegal immigration, if it hurts anyone at all, harms legal immigrants and other citizens at the bottom of the economic ladder, whose opportunities are taken and wages depressed by the presence of illegal workers. Schwarzenegger could say all these things and yet not be accused of bashing immigrants, because he was one. At times, indeed, he said all of them. But he never did so consistently, and rarely with the kind of passion and eloquence that would cause voters to take notice and agree.

At first it almost seemed as if Schwarzenegger wanted to avoid the issue. He came into his first campaign tainted in the eyes of many Hispanics because he had supported Proposition 187, the anti-immigrant ballot measure that his mentor, former governor Pete Wilson, made the centerpiece of his own reelection campaign in 1994. That measure sought to end most public services to illegal immigrants, including education and health care, except in emergencies. Although it passed easily, most of Proposition 187 was thrown out by a federal court. But its legacy was more political than legal. The nasty campaign waged on its behalf made many Latinos wary of Republicans and the Republican Party. Schwarzenegger later backed away from his position on 187, saying he would never agree to deny education to children, no matter what their immigration status.[1] But few heard that explanation, and his opponents in the race for governor played up his ties to Wilson and the anti-immigration proposal.

Schwarzenegger, as a candidate in 2003, was also on the run from media reports questioning his own early immigration status. The *San Jose Mercury News* published stories suggesting that Schwarzenegger, as a young immigrant from Austria, might have worked illegally, in violation of the terms of a special, limited visa he was originally given to enter the country. The implications were potentially explosive: Was the man running for governor as a critic of illegal immigration a former illegal immigrant himself? Dion Nissenbaum, the *Mercury News* reporter who wrote the stories, followed Schwarzenegger to his public events for weeks, asking him to release his immigration records to the public. Schwarzenegger ignored him—and the allegation was never confirmed.

But as the campaign unfolded, Schwarzenegger could not resist jumping into the debate over an immigration issue that had become red hot in car-crazy California: driver's licenses. During its last big wave of anti-immigration fervor, California had banned licenses for illegal immigrants in 1993. Many Democrats and even some Latinos supported that legislation. But now Latinos in the Legislature were trying to repeal the law and make citizenship status no longer an issue in the granting of driver's licenses. They argued that it was a matter of safety. Illegal immigrants were going to drive anyway, advocates said. Allowing them to get licenses would at least force them to learn the rules of the road, and it would qualify them to buy insurance. Everyone would benefit from that. The insurance industry and many law enforcement groups agreed, and they supported the move. But it was highly controversial.

Although illegal immigration was not the hot-button issue it had been in the 1990s, the idea of granting new benefits to illegal immigrants was not popular. Governor Davis tried to dodge the issue. He vetoed the first bill that reached his desk,[2] calling it "an invitation to fraud," and two years later he rejected another, this time laying out a series of reasons why he was opposed.[3] The eternally cautious chief executive knew that the issue was radioactive, and he didn't want any part of it. In 2002, after Davis issued his second veto, Latinos in the Legislature accused him of acting in bad faith, and they withdrew their endorsement for his reelection, an extraordinary step to take against a fellow Democrat.

In the midst of the recall election the next year, however, Davis needed the support of old friends. In his desperation, he was willing to gamble. Assemblyman Gilbert Cedillo, the Legislature's biggest advocate for the issue, fashioned yet another bill that allowed any immigrant, legal or illegal, to get a license. Even though the measure lacked the security safeguards and other requirements on which Davis had insisted, the governor signed it. His action prompted an uproar on the right, among anti-immigration groups and the conservative talk radio hosts for whom illegal immigration was a bread-and-butter issue. A poll would later show that about 70 percent of California voters opposed giving licenses to illegal immigrants. Schwarzenegger's campaign saw those poll numbers, and the governor's willingness to defy them, as a gift from heaven.

The candidate quickly seized on the issue. He said the bill was wrong, and he pledged, if elected, to push for its repeal. "I think it is ridiculous," Schwarzenegger said on *Fox News*.[4] "It's unsafe for the state. It creates big security problems here. The law enforcement community is against that. The federal government is against that. The attorney general of California, Bill Lockyer, is against that, and I am definitely against it."

That was all the conservatives heard, and that was enough for them. But those who were paying close attention heard a little bit more. Schwarzenegger, as he often does, left the door open for something more creative, and more moderate. He suggested he wanted to repeal the bill and replace it with another piece of legislation that would allow illegal immigrants to get a license, with some conditions and safeguards. No one really knew what that meant, and Schwarzenegger never explained it fully.

Once he took office, however, Schwarzenegger seemed to conclude that he could not afford the conservative backlash that would result if he fulfilled that vague pledge. As promised, he persuaded the Legislature to repeal the law, which lawmakers did knowing that voters would almost certainly act if they did not. With the law off the books, illegal immigrants were back where they started: unable to get licenses. But Schwarzenegger met with Cedillo in the governor's private office in Santa Monica, and the lawmaker came away with the impression that the new governor had committed to replacing the repealed law with a new one that would allow at least some undocumented immigrants to get licenses. Perhaps it would apply only to those who were working; perhaps to those who were seeking legal status. Applicants would have to undergo some sort of background check. Cedillo, who by then had become a state senator, would try for three years to nail Schwarzenegger down on the terms of that agreement, but to no avail.

At one point, Schwarzenegger explained it this way on a San Diego radio show:

"I went to the original sponsor that took it through and had it passed—it was Senator Cedillo—and I said, 'Why don't you get rid of this, and let's then afterwards do it the right way, so that California can feel safe, let's do it with the background check, and let's do it with insurance and all that.' And so, that's what we worked out.

"So, now we are trying to figure out a way of how can we do that, and there are many, many people who are working on that, that are studying it, how we can bring all those things together so that California is safe while we are giving driver's licenses to people that are going to work. So, that's really what the whole thing is about. That's what we're working on right now."[5]

That was in February 2004, just a few months after he took office. But the discussions went nowhere. Cedillo had promised his wife on her deathbed that he would stay with the issue until he succeeded, and he focused so much on the quest that he became known around the Capitol as "one-bill Gil." After a while, though, it became clear even to him that Schwarzenegger was simply treading water, hoping that the issue would go away. Cedillo persuaded his colleagues to pass yet another bill toward the end of 2004, but Schwarzenegger vetoed it. After that, the immigration issue faded into the background for many months. Schwarzenegger rarely mentioned it, and he did little to reach out to the Latino community. Unlike his predecessor, he seemed in no hurry to visit Mexico, nor to meet with that nation's president.

But as 2005 dawned and Schwarzenegger took on a tougher, more confrontational persona on issues across the board, he returned to immigration with vigor. Speaking to a group of newspaper editors meeting in San Francisco in the spring of 2005, Schwarzenegger suddenly abandoned his cautious approach and veered toward the anti-immigration side, sounding, if nothing else, like his old friend Pete Wilson, who had once referred to the influx of immigrants as an "invasion."

"Close the borders in California, all across Mexico and the United States," Schwarzenegger told the editors in a statement that shocked his audience. It surprised his staff, too.[6]

Even before the governor left the hall, his spokeswoman, Margita Thompson, scurried to the press bay to tell reporters that Schwarzenegger hadn't meant what he said. The next day, he apologized. "Instead of closing, I meant securing," Schwarzenegger said. "I think maybe my English, I need to go back to school and study a little bit."[7]

But Schwarzenegger did not go back to school. He went on the radio, on KFI in Los Angeles, where talk show hosts John Kobylt and Ken Chiampou—known to their listeners as John and Ken—made a living stoking the emotions of Southern Californians upset about illegal immigration. Their latest crusade was aimed at a billboard placed along major Los Angeles freeways to promote a Spanish-language television station. The ads showed the LA skyline dominated by a prominent Mexico City landmark, a golden angel. "Your news, your team. Los Angeles, CA," the billboard said. But the two-letter abbreviation for "California" was crossed out and replaced by "Mexico." This metaphorical merging of north and south, California and Mexico, was an affront to John, Ken, and their listeners, who considered the ad another example of the "reconquistador" plot to retake the southwestern United States for Mexico.

The governor heard about the controversy and decided to weigh in. Schwarzenegger placed a call to the show, on which he was a frequent guest, and complained about the billboards. He told the radio hosts that he considered the ads "extremely divisive" and unnecessary.

"The big mistake is that it promotes illegal aliens to come in here, and it's the last thing we need," he said, bungling his English a bit. But his meaning was clear enough. "They should take it down immediately," he said.

If that had been all the governor had said, the incident would have passed with little notice. But once the hosts had Schwarzenegger on their show, talking immigration, they couldn't resist the opportunity to see how far he would go. So they asked him about the Minutemen, a self-appointed group of citizen border-patrollers who were walking the line in Arizona in what they said was an attempt to frighten illegal immigrants away from crossing over. The group planned to expand the operation to California, and their leader, Jim Gilchrist, was running for Congress in an Orange County race to fill a seat that opened up when the incumbent was appointed by President Bush to a federal job. Bush had called the group "vigilantes." But Schwarzenegger saw it differently.

"I think they have done a terrific job and they have, look, they have cut down the crossing of illegal immigrants by a huge percentage, so it just shows that it works when you go and make an effort and when you work hard," the governor said. He compared them to neighborhood watch groups and said he didn't blame them for trying to do a job the federal government had neglected.[8]

The comments, of course, drew an immediate outcry from immigrant rights activists, legislators, and others. Hector De La Torre, a Democratic legislator from Los Angeles County, described the governor's comments as "the rantings of a desperate politician" and an effort "to scapegoat people" who were down. "This isn't an action movie," De La Torre said. "It isn't cool that there are people out in the desert with guns."

Art Torres, chairman of the California Democratic Party, was just as quick to pounce. "It is illegal to interfere with law enforcement, and if the governor is promoting that, then maybe we should think of bringing action against him," Torres said. "When he took an oath of office to defend and protect the Constitution of the United States, that includes all of its laws. And when the president of the United States and the Border Patrol both suggest that these activities are not only not helpful, but possibly illegal, that needs to be seriously examined."[9]

This time, Schwarzenegger didn't back down from his comment, though his press aides did try to shift attention from the private patrols to the federal government, which they alleged was not doing its job. But the Minutemen controversy slowly faded on its own, and once again the governor let the emotional issue recede into the political woodwork. As quickly as his interest in immigration had spiked, it dissipated. Congress, meanwhile, was about to let him off the hook on the driver's license issue.

In June 2005, Republicans in Congress tacked onto an Iraq war funding bill something called the "Real ID Act," which was aimed at making sure the driver's license was a reliable and secure form of identification for boarding commercial airplanes or entering federal buildings. The Act required all states to use uniform procedures for issuing licenses, and it banned the issuance of regular driver's licenses to illegal immigrants. The law did allow states to give licenses to illegal immigrants that would permit them to drive but that could not be used as legal identification for federal purposes, including boarding airline flights. But the federal regulations fleshing out the law would not be written for years, and Schwarzenegger used the new law as an excuse to avoid the issue for the rest of his first term. When Cedillo returned one more time with a bill he described as an implementation of the new federal law, Schwarzenegger vetoed that one, too.

By the time Congress took up the broader immigration issue again in 2006, Schwarzenegger had resurrected his more moderate instincts on the subject. His tone began to change, and he sounded more inclusive, less angry. But he still had trouble coming down firmly either for or against specific policy proposals.

He did flatly oppose a proposal by Republicans in Congress to make illegal immigration a felony. On the other hand, he also said he opposed what he called "amnesty" for illegal immigrants. At first he took no position on a provision being discussed that would have given undocumented aliens the opportunity to gain resident status and eventually citizenship, which many immigration opponents considered amnesty by another name. And while Schwarzenegger said fences along the border should be part of any solution, he did not endorse a proposal for 700 miles of fencing that was in a House bill and was being considered in the Senate. Pressed on the details during an exchange with the press, he ducked. "I'll let the geniuses in Washington," he said at one point, "figure all that out."[10]

As the year wore on, Schwarzenegger eventually fleshed out his position. It reflected, he said, his long-standing belief that the country needed both to secure its borders and to provide a way for more people to immigrate legally, and for more businesses to find foreign workers when they needed them. His call for border security appealed to those on the right who were upset by illegal immigration. His support for expanded guest-worker programs was popular with employers and with that segment of the left that favored a more liberal immigration policy. And he mixed in a patriotic call for immigrants to assimilate with a plea for tolerance from the Anglo population, a position that seemed both heartfelt and designed to appeal to centrist voters.

Schwarzenegger's response to Bush's request for National Guard troops at the border was typical of his search for middle ground. At first the governor called the president's plan "half-baked" and gave the impression that he might not go along. He sent the White House a memo demanding answers to a series of questions about the deployment, its cost, and how long it would last. But even before he got the answers he was seeking, Schwarzenegger complied and ordered the troops to the border. He eventually nailed down most of his concerns in a memorandum of understanding with the federal government. Then he visited the border, did a photo op with the soldiers, and praised their commitment to the mission.

At the same time, Schwarzenegger began to support a bipartisan movement in Congress for a comprehensive immigration reform bill. In an opinion piece published in the *Los Angeles Times*, he spelled out his position in more detail then ever before:

> The answer, as I have repeatedly said, is, first, to secure the border to stop the problem from getting worse. Second, we must create a temporary-worker program so people can come here legally to work. We should also lift the cap on work visas for industries such as technology, engineering and agriculture so immigrants can be hired when there are not enough U.S. workers. And we must create a path to legal status for those living in the shadows illegally. They must pay a fine for breaking our laws. They must learn English and become part of our culture. They must pay back taxes and pay for health care and education rather than expect American taxpayers to pay extra when some cannot even afford health care or college for their own children.

Schwarzenegger opposed any plan to try to send back the 12 million immigrants believed to be in the country illegally. But he also had stern words for people at both edges of the emotional debate. In a private conversation with one of his speech writers that was taped and later made public, Schwarzenegger compared Mexican immigrants to "squatters" in Zimbabwe and to houseguests who refuse to help with the chores. After Schwarzenegger's staff realized that his Democratic opponent had a copy of the recording, he gave a speech that reflected his private comments and expanded on them in an opinion piece.

Immigrants, he wrote, were like "guests" in somebody's home who had an obligation to do more than "sit on the couch." They must try to participate in civil society, he said, and assimilate into the American fabric. Schwarzenegger, in comparing the assimilation of Mexican immigrants with that of the Europeans and Asians who preceded them, probably exaggerated the degree to which earlier generations had shed their native cultures, and understated the degree to which Mexicans and other Latin Americans were embracing the culture of the United States even as they influenced it with their own social mores. But his words were chosen carefully to tap into the mainstream's desire to see immigrants accepted into American culture while embracing their new society as their own:

> What people see today when immigrant rights activists march in the streets carrying Mexican flags and angry signs is that you do not want to join America's house. The message that sends is that you do not want to learn our language or our culture. Unlike the message sent by the masses of Irish, Italian, German and Asian immigrants, whom Americans now proudly call our "melting pot," these images suggest that Mexican immigrants do not want to make that effort.
>
> I do not believe that this is the message most Mexican immigrants—legal or illegal—wish to send. I believe that most Mexican immigrants are as proud to be part of America as I was. They are some of the hardest working and strongest believers in the American dream. So my message to you is: Carry your home country in your heart, but carry the American flag in our streets.

He also warned those on the right not to scapegoat immigrants: "To those who believe illegal immigration is reaching a crisis level in this country I say: Tone down the rhetoric. I myself have said things that caused division even when that was not my intent. Words can be weapons. We must be careful to distinguish between legal and illegal immigration, between those who break our laws to do us harm and those who break our laws to find freedom and prosperity in the greatest nation on Earth."

Schwarzenegger—and his writing staff—had finally found his voice. He had found a mature, civil way to discuss an emotional issue. And he was in sync with the voters. Polls showed that more than half of California adults believed that immigrants were more of a benefit than a burden to society, and 70 percent believed illegal immigrants should be able to remain in the country if they were working.

But if Schwarzenegger's language had become clearer, the thoughts were essentially the same as the ones with which he had begun his political career. He was back where he started.

In September 2003, when asked to explain his position opposing driver's licenses for illegal immigrants, Schwarzenegger had told the *Sacramento Bee* that he wanted to find a way to make illegal immigrants legal residents—and then give them the right to drive.

"Check their backgrounds; check for criminal activities," Schwarzenegger said. "Those who have not been involved . . . let them work rather than having to hide and worry. Let them work in the farms and the construction sites and all this because there's great workers out there. The idea is not to send them home. The idea is not to split the families. That's all nonsense."[11]

If he had simply kept hammering on that theme instead of wandering around in the immigration wilderness, the public would have had a much better understanding of where he stood all along.

THIRTEEN

Justice Delayed

When Schwarzenegger took office in November of 2003, he was in a perfect position to try to fix the state's sprawling prison system. Thanks to his career in the movies, Schwarzenegger, for better or worse, had a public persona as a guy who mowed down villains like a machine. His first career as a body builder, moreover, still gave him an image of strength, decades after he relinquished his last crown as Mr. Universe. Neither of those things should have counted in how the voters viewed his performance as governor. But they did. And that gave him leeway to conduct a rational evaluation and overhaul of criminal justice policy without being seen as soft on crime.

Schwarzenegger fumbled the opportunity. Time after time he moved in the direction of reform, but each time he pulled back, his deeds never living up to his words. Finally, midway through 2007— the first year of his second term—he helped broker a compromise in the Legislature that he hailed as the most significant change in criminal justice policy in California in a generation. In classic "post-partisan" fashion, the new law promised a major expansion of the prison system to relieve overcrowding in the short term, coupled with a renewed focus on rehabilitation to keep ex-cons from committing new crimes after they were released from prison. The plan won wide support in the Legislature from both Republicans and

Democrats. But by then Schwarzenegger had squandered his credibility on the issue, and few independent observers believed that his administration would or could actually implement the law in a way that would live up to its promise. Even some of those who voted for the deal said they thought it would probably lead to nothing.

Things didn't begin that way for Schwarzenegger. Although his experience with prison issues was limited to his forays inside them to teach bodybuilding to the inmates, he recognized shortly after taking office that the state's broken prison system was a major problem that had been festering for years, and he set out to fix it. He brought in a respected former governor—Republican George Deukmejian—to head a bipartisan commission to study the prisons. Deukmejian was an inspired choice, because he was, arguably, the father of the largest prison building boom in the nation's history, which began in the 1980s and stretched until 1995. Under Deukmejian and his successors, California lengthened prison sentences and made it tougher for inmates to earn good-time credits, pushing up the population of people behind bars from 22,000 in 1980 to 160,000 by the time Schwarzenegger took office in 2003. To hold all those criminals, the state built 21 new prisons, and the prison department budget exploded from $1 billion to nearly $10 billion a year, more than the state spent on the University of California and the California State University systems combined.

But lately even Deukmejian had begun to ponder whether the state could sustain what he had wrought. And his commission's report, about nine months into Schwarzenegger's first term, was an honest assessment that laid bare the problems and offered a number of provocative solutions.

The problems were clear enough. Spurred in part by the rush to lengthen sentences, but also by a prison system that lacked any incentives for criminals to improve their lives and a parole system that was dysfunctional at best, California had a terrible record when it came to the rate at which ex-cons re-offended and ended up back behind bars. About 70 percent of the inmates who left the state's prisons were back within three years, because they either violated the conditions of their parole or committed new crimes.

The result was a prison system that was nearly bursting. Built to handle 82,000 inmates, by the time Schwarzenegger took office it was holding twice that many. Even with double-celling, which is commonplace in prisons across the country, the system was still holding thousands more inmates than it could safely contain. More than 17,000 prisoners were stuffed into gymnasiums, classrooms, and hallways. Violence was rampant, and the crowding took up space that should have been going toward education and drug treatment. Even people who didn't feel sorry for the inmates worried that the conditions might prompt the federal courts to order the state to stop adding more prisoners. That could force the release of felons from prison early or stop the transfer of convicted criminals from local jails, causing more overcrowding there.

If the problem was easy to describe, however, the solutions were more elusive, especially given the hyperpartisan atmosphere that typically surrounded the issue of crime and punishment in America. Historically, Republicans favored what they saw as tougher criminal justice policies. They didn't believe rehabilitation worked, and they wanted only to build more prisons to accommodate the growing number of inmates. But Democrats opposed adding more space, in part because they would rather have spent the money on other things. They also believed the state's criminal justice system was too bent on incarceration and not focused enough on turning around at least the handful of inmates who were open to change. That stalemate meant the state was neither building new prisons nor doing anything to reduce the number of inmates. The general public didn't care, as long as the problem remained out of sight. They didn't want to think about the fact that most of the people in prison would eventually be released, or that when the prisoners got out they would be more hardened and less prepared to deal with the civilized world than when they had gone in. It was a recipe for disaster.

The Deukmejian Commission's recommendations were sweeping, and they would have placed California on the cutting edge of rehabilitation—had they been followed. The most radical idea on the list was a plan to junk the state's sentencing system, which was based on fixed terms for each crime, and replace it with a more flexible structure that would allow inmates to earn their way out of prison early with their behavior. The state's rigid sentencing system had been in place since the 1970s, when a coalition of liberals upset about racial disparities and conservatives who believed judges were being too lenient combined to adopt a system of set terms or ranges within which judges could work. But that change had two very big unintended consequences. First, it prompted a bidding war as legislators sought to out-tough each other by lengthening mandatory minimum sentences for one crime after another, often after an unusually heinous crime made statewide or national news. Second, the fixed terms gave inmates no incentive to change their behavior. Under the old system, they had to earn parole by showing remorse and making a case that they could return to the streets without committing new crimes. Now they simply did their time and were dumped back into their communities, no matter how dangerous they might still be. Although they could earn a day off their terms for every day worked in prison or spent in school, there were no performance standards or individual expectations that each inmate could meet to earn his release.

The Deukmejian proposal called for the state to perform a detailed evaluation of every inmate as he entered the system and to develop a plan for education, job training, and substance abuse treatment tailored to that inmate. If an inmate completed the program prepared for him, and met required benchmarks, he would serve a far shorter sentence—perhaps only half as long as the maximum allowed by law.

The panel also proposed expanding prerelease programs that connected inmates to the community with job counseling, housing referrals, and substance-abuse treatment. And it recommended the expansion of a new parole model already under way that offered more programs for ex-cons and let more of them remain in the community, under supervision, even if they violated the conditions of their parole by, for example, failing a drug test. Instead of sending them back to prison, the new model would confine them to their homes with electronic monitoring or put them into drug treatment in the community.

But the commission's recommendations, issued midway through 2004, were swallowed up in the Department of Corrections bureaucracy. While Schwarzenegger won legislative approval to reorganize the corrections agency and change its name—officially adding "rehabilitation" as part of its public mission—he made little progress in changing the department's policies. The state couldn't add more education and training because it had cut staff to save money. It couldn't add more drug treatment because it didn't have the space or the money to hire counselors. And it couldn't free up space as long as Schwarzenegger refused to consider sentencing reform or even the idea of letting seemingly harmless geriatric inmates out of prison before the end of their scheduled terms.

In fact, Schwarzenegger actually retreated. Under pressure from the powerful prison guards union, which also represented parole agents, he abruptly dropped the new parole model because agents claimed they were being forced to leave dangerous criminals in the community. At the time he abandoned the initiative, a crime-victims group backed by the prison guards union was running television ads criticizing Schwarzenegger and warning that he was putting public safety at risk. His top prison official, Rod

Hickman, told the Legislature that the program was dropped because it wasn't working as envisioned. There was some evidence of
that—mainly because the programs that were supposed to divert
parolees from prison weren't ready, so violators were being let off
the hook but not given the counseling or other help that was meant
to set them straight. But inmate rights advocates concluded that
the administration simply could not take the political heat.

The affair exposed Schwarzenegger's strange relationship with
the correctional officers' union, which had grown over the past 20
years, along with the prison system, until it was one of the most
powerful labor organizations in the state. The California Correctional Peace Officers Association, now more than 30,000 members
strong, had contributed or spent hundreds of thousands of dollars
on behalf of each of the past two governors, one a Republican, one
a Democrat. The union also donated generously to legislators of
both parties. But Schwarzenegger, during the recall campaign, had
distanced himself from them, refusing to take their money and la-
beling the union one of the "special interests" he sought to sweep
from the Capitol.

After he took office, Schwarzenegger lobbied the Legislature to
break the guards' last contract with the state, a five-year deal that
gave the officers a 37 percent pay raise and significant new powers
over the operation of the prisons. The governor argued that the
contract was passed under false pretenses because the Legislature
was not fully aware of its provisions, and it included a standard
clause that said the raises would take place each year only if there
were sufficient money in the state's budget. With the treasury running a multibillion-dollar deficit, he said, California couldn't afford
the deal. But the Democrats in the Legislature refused to go along,
and the contract held. Schwarzenegger settled for a face-saving re-
vision that delayed the raises but allowed them to go forward as
planned. Even to get that concession, he agreed to many of the
union's demands, including a guarantee that the union would get

access to videotapes of inmate violence, which the union used in a
television advertising campaign to persuade voters and politicians
that the guards walked the "toughest beat" in the state.

But the agreement to delay the raises did not end the tension
between the governor and the union. After the Deukmejian Commission cited the union's influence as part of the problem in the
prisons, Schwarzenegger took up that charge as well, and in his annual speech to the Legislature in January 2005 he attacked the
guards directly.

"This is an agency in which there has been too much political influence, too much union control and too little management courage
and accountability," Schwarzenegger said. "For many months, you
could not pick up a newspaper without reading about a youth dying
in prison, or codes of silence, or abuses of force. I want to put the
corrupt people in our prisons on the same side of the bars."

Those were fighting words, and the union took them as such.
The organization not only challenged Schwarzenegger's prison
policies but helped lead the opposition to the series of broader government reforms he pushed in 2005. At one rally on the steps of the
Capitol, the president of the prison guards union embraced the
president of the California Teachers Association in a huge bear hug,
an especially significant gesture because the two organizations
were historic rivals, fighting over their share of the budget and
rarely agreeing on anything.

After Susan Kennedy joined the administration as Schwarzenegger's second chief of staff, she tried to calm the waters.
According to Kennedy, she simply concluded that it would be impossible for Schwarzenegger to reform the prisons if he remained
at war with the union, because it had the ability to block much of
what he was trying to do. The parties, she said, at least had to get
back on speaking terms, and she began to meet with union officials, as did Schwarzenegger. But those meetings spurred specula-
tion that the union was now running the show in the Department of

Corrections, and first one, then another head of the prison agency resigned. A special investigator for the federal courts accused the governor of cozying up to the union, and even suggested that some of his aides may have broken the law in doing so.

That watchdog—John Hagar—said Schwarzenegger had backed down after "one of the most productive periods of prison reform," in the state's history. Hagar said the governor had given the union a "disturbing" amount of power in the day-to-day decisions of the agency.

"Integrity and remedial plan efforts must begin at the top, and then percolate down," Hagar, who was known as the court's "special master," wrote in his report. "Beginning January 2006, however, it appears that the requisite leadership has been absent from the governor's office. Evidence before the special master indicates that the governor's office may have given the code of silence in California's prisons a new lease on life."[1]

Despite the alleged collaboration, however, the union went on to endorse Schwarzenegger's opponent in his reelection bid, and it produced and aired ads attacking the governor. But after threatening to spend as much as $10 million on commercials opposing him, the union quietly backed off and eventually spent only a fraction of that amount. It appeared at first that the union was going easy on Schwarzenegger in exchange for his commitment to give them another fat new contract, but the sides remained at impasse on that issue well into Schwarzenegger's second term. Somehow, though, Schwarzenegger had managed to appear as if he was on the take to an interest group from which he had never taken a dime.

The governor, meanwhile, inserted himself into two ballot fights that had the effect of driving the prison population even higher. He campaigned against a measure that would have changed the state's "Three Strikes" sentencing law, which sent two-time felons back to prison for 25 years to life on their third felony conviction. Opponents of the law had tried to soften it so that only those con-

victed of a third serious or violent crime—rather than any felony—
would face life behind bars. The reform measure was ahead in the
polls until Schwarzenegger joined several former governors (and
the prison guards union) in a last-minute, high-profile campaign to
defeat it.

He was also a big backer of "Jessica's Law," a ballot measure
that would require lifetime electronic monitoring of paroled sex
offenders and prohibit them from living near schools or parks.
Some law enforcement officials complained that the law was
poorly written and would mean a huge increase in workload for little or no gain in public safety, since there was no evidence that
parolees who lived near schools or parks were any more likely to
re-offend than those who lived elsewhere. Prosecutors in other
states where similar laws had been tried said the measures actually
made the public less safe, because they prompted parolees to go
underground and stop registering with the police. If they did follow
the law and move away from urban areas, they were likely to be
distant from families and professional support that was crucial in
preventing them from returning to their former ways. But Schwarzenegger wouldn't heed any of those arguments, and with his enthusiastic support, the measure passed easily.

All of this was popular with Republicans and helped prop up the
shaky right flank of Schwarzenegger's political coalition. But it only
promised to make his prison problems worse.

When Schwarzenegger took office, there were about 161,000 inmates in California's prisons, and that number was projected to decline to about 148,000 by July 2005, thanks mainly to the parole reforms that were then just getting started. But by the summer of
2007, the prison population not only had not declined, it had grown
to more than 170,000, and by then was projected to grow another
20,000 in the years ahead.

In 2005, a federal court judge in San Francisco took over the
prison health system, declaring that the medical care the state was

providing to inmates did not meet the minimum standard required by the Constitution. He later appointed a receiver to run the system and gave him the ability to override state civil service rules, contracting regulations, and any other impediment he might find in his way. Another court was monitoring mental health care in the prisons, and a third kept an eye on the treatment of inmates with disabilities. By 2007, all three courts were eying the rising inmate population. In July, two of the judges triggered a legal process that could lead to a cap on the prison population, forcing the state to release some inmates early or stop accepting new transfers from the counties.

Schwarzenegger called a special session of the Legislature in 2006 and asked for authority to build at least two new prisons while beefing up the system's rehabilitation programs. But the Legislature rejected his plan and offered nothing in its place. The governor then declared an emergency and began transferring inmates to other states to relieve overcrowding. But the correctional officers and another state employees union sued, arguing that the governor lacked the authority to take that action without approval from the Legislature. A lower court agreed. In January of 2007, Schwarzenegger tried again, proposing a new expansion plan coupled with still more reforms.

"Here are the court-ordered choices we face: We build more prisons or we release criminals," Schwarzenegger told the Legislature. "We build more prisons or the court takes the money from education and health care and builds the prisons itself. Now I am not in favor of releasing criminals. Nor am I in favor of taking money from classrooms and emergency rooms to build cells. Where do you stand? We must act. And we must act this year."[2]

Finally, the governor began to get some traction. His latest plan was better balanced than his earlier efforts, and Democratic lawmakers, fearing a court takeover, signaled that they would probably agree to some kind of deal. Schwarzenegger then began taking a lower public profile, allowing legislative leaders from both parties to negotiate a compromise behind the scenes while his staff monitored it from the sidelines. In late April 2007, lawmakers reached a deal, and the governor announced that he would sign it. It was rushed through the Assembly and Senate before the guards union and other opponents had a chance to stop it. The unions mounted a determined challenge, but with the leadership of both parties on board, the plan could not be stopped.[3]

The compromise had something for everybody. The governor and Republican lawmakers got added space in the prisons, though not as much as they wanted. The final deal called for adding 40,000 new prison beds and 13,000 county jail beds. Of the state's share, about 16,000 would be built in existing prisons, just enough to replace all the beds then occupying temporary space in day rooms and gymnasiums. Another 16,000 would be at new, mostly urban "re-entry" centers for inmates serving the end of their sentences, and 8,000 were to be for sick and mentally ill inmates.

The Democrats, meanwhile, demanded and received significant concessions on rehabilitation, although much of what they got were things Schwarzenegger had promised to do in the past but never delivered. The re-entry centers, for example, had long been part of the governor's proposals, but now the sides agreed on a number of beds, a funding source (borrowed money), and a plan for their programs. Inmates with less than a year to serve on their sentences would be sent to the centers, where they would be closer to their families and receive intensive help aimed at finding them a job and a place to live when they got out.

The program also included the addition of 4,000 new slots for drug treatment in the prisons and a commitment to provide the crucial aftercare to inmates once they left prison. The same was true for mental health: Schwarzenegger agreed to establish day treatment and crisis centers for parolees. The state would also conduct the kind of full screening of every new inmate recommended by the Deukmejian Commission, with the information gleaned through that process used to create a custom-fit program aimed at reducing recidivism. To relieve the pressure on the system immediately, Schwarzenegger was also given the authority to transfer as many as 8,000 inmates to other states.

Given Schwarzenegger's lack of credibility on the issue, the Legislature also insisted that the new beds be added in two phases, with the second phase not allowed to begin unless the state had first fulfilled its commitment to add education, training, and drug programs.

The deal did not include a sentencing commission, but Democrats believed that Schwarzenegger would eventually agree to one. He told reporters that, on that issue, "everything is on the table."[4] And while no major parole reforms were included—other than the new services to be provided—Schwarzenegger's aides said they were moving to begin discharging ex-cons from parole supervision after 12 months (instead of 3 years) if they committed no new crimes and stayed drug-free.

Many legislators said they voted for the bill only in hopes of staving off a federal takeover, which would have been worse. They said they had little confidence in Schwarzenegger's administration to carry out its provisions.

"There's not a Democrat here this morning that likes this vote, that likes this bill," said the Senate's Democratic leader, Don Perata of Oakland. "I don't know how the governor will pull this off, but I sure think we can sell tickets to watch. . . . This tests any article of faith that I've ever been associated with. I do not, as I stand here, believe this job can get done."[5]

But others said it was a sincere effort to change the entire culture of the prison system.

"This is not business as usual in California," said James Tilton, Schwarzenegger's secretary of Corrections and Rehabilitation. "In spite of what many people think, most inmates come back out of the prison system into communities. This is an opportunity to partner with local communities, to build local beds for inmates who are either on parole in their communities, or coming out of the prison system into their communities. Instead of just delivering them to that county with $200 and a bus ticket, we're going to deliver inmates who have got assessments of their individual needs in terms of services, provide programs that meet those individual needs, so that when inmates come out they have a chance to deal with their drug treatment, deal with anger management, education skills, have a chance to get a job and be successful."[6]

Joan Petersilia, a University of California, Irvine, professor who is an expert on criminal justice and California's problems, had a more nuanced take. Petersilia, a frequent critic of the administration who also worked with the prisons to implement reforms, noted that every year, the state sent 120,000 inmates back behind bars. Not many of them could be diverted, she said, but if only a few could be kept straight, the savings would be tremendous. The legislation, she said, would have been much better had it included more serious reform of the parole system to keep nonviolent, low-level violators from being continuously recycled into and out of prison. But she held out hope that the moves it did make toward rehabilitation would be successful.

The bill, she said, focused the prisons on "not simply serving as a transfer place, but a transition place. And we've got to get people better prepared to return home. I think the best science that we can bring to this will reduce recidivism about 10 percent. . . . If we could just simply reduce the intake . . . if we can reduce that by just 6,000 to 10,000 a year, those programs pay for themselves at least tenfold."[7]

If Petersilia's hopes are realized, it could lead to a transformation of the prison system that would stand as one of Schwarzenegger's greatest accomplishments. But there was nothing in his record on the issue before he signed that bill to suggest that he would follow through and make the kind of tough decisions it would take to change the culture of the prisons, to turn them from criminal finishing schools into places where at least a few convicts who were willing to change were given the chance and the incentive to do so before returning to the streets. And if the bill, as its critics feared, results in more prison beds, more crowding, higher costs, and one more failed effort to overhaul the criminal justice system, Schwarzenegger will deserve much of the blame.

FOURTEEN

Going to School

Schwarzenegger's approach to education policy can best be captured by the story of Eli Williams, the American Civil Liberties Union, and their lawsuit against the state of California.

Schwarzenegger, it is safe to say, is no fan of the ACLU. Like most Republicans, he differs with the civil rights group on matters ranging from criminal sentencing to affirmative action. But when, as a private citizen in 2000, he read that the ACLU was suing the state over the condition of its schools, the case—and the cause—rang true for him.

Eli Williams was a seventh grader at Luther Burbank Middle School in San Francisco and the lead plaintiff in the lawsuit that took his name. The Williams case claimed that school buildings in 18 districts around the state were poorly maintained, falling apart, and infested with rats. Without proper heating, cooling, and ventilation, the rooms were often too cold in the winter and too hot in summer. Furthermore, the students and their lawyers argued, their classrooms lacked current textbooks, and their teachers lacked full credentials. "The conditions are so bad that if these schools were prisons, they would be shut down," said ACLU attorney Peter Eliasberg, who worked on the suit.[1]

Although the conditions alleged in the lawsuit were, strictly speaking, the purview of local school districts, the lawsuit was filed against the state. The litigants wanted the state to step in and provide more money, more oversight, or both, to do whatever it took to ensure a clean, safe, and professional learning environment for the students. Ultimately, they said, the state should set standards for classroom conditions just as it had for academics.

Governor Gray Davis, however, had other ideas. Convinced that the state was not responsible for the problems and that losing would prove costly to the taxpayers, Davis approved the hiring of a pricey private law firm, O'Melvany and Myers, to fight the suit. The firm countersued the local school districts on the state's behalf, and its lawyers began taking depositions from potential witnesses, including students as young as eight years old. Some of the students complained about the interviews, saying they had been intimidated and verbally abused. While the students were represented for free by the ACLU and a San Francisco firm doing the work pro bono, O'Melvany and Myers billed the state $325 an hour for its lawyers—a tab that eventually came to more than $18 million.

"He's Scrooge Davis," said Wayne Johnson, who was president of the California Teachers Association at the time. "The ACLU tries to get poor kids some semblance of what others get, and Davis fights them like a wounded tiger. It's abominable."[2]

Davis was reelected a year later. A year after that, he was recalled from office. But the lawsuit ground on. Enter Schwarzenegger.

Bonnie Reiss, his friend and adviser, said that she and Schwarzenegger first learned of the ACLU lawsuit while flying to a meeting for his Inner-City Games Foundation shortly after the suit was filed in 2000. Reiss brought a newspaper along on the plane, and, flipping through it, happened to see a news article about the Williams case. She showed it to Schwarzenegger, and they both were intrigued by the ACLU's argument. They had seen conditions similar to those described in the lawsuit in their tours of urban schools as part of their work for Schwarzenegger's foundation.

At the time, Schwarzenegger says, as he shuttled between schools in Beverly Hills that had everything, and the broken down, poorly equipped campuses in the poor community of Compton a few miles to the south, he wondered why California allowed such disparities.

"Some schools get great teachers, other schools get less qualified teachers," he said. "Some schools have great school buildings, other schools don't."[3] When he ran for governor, he committed himself to trying to address the problem. After he was elected and he learned that the Williams lawsuit was still pending, he immediately pulled the private lawyers off the case. Reiss called the ACLU and arranged for a private meeting in Schwarzenegger's smoking tent to begin negotiations to settle the lawsuit. After four years of battling a Democratic governor, the group's lawyers were thrilled to be sitting down with a Republican chief executive who shared their goals.

"It was a discussion about problem solving," said Mark Rosenbaum, one of the ACLU lawyers who attended that first meeting. "The principle was that all kids should have access to what they needed to succeed. His position was that, under his administration, there was not going to be a kid who did not have the books he or she needed in school. It was clear this was organic to who he was. He was personally engaged at a primal level."[4]

Schwarzenegger later described the negotiations from his point of view. "You have to give equal education, equal opportunities, to every child," he said. "I couldn't wait to get in there and sit down with all the stakeholders and settle the case. It was very clear, these are not unreasonable people. The ACLU is not like an organization that I would naturally gravitate to, but they were absolutely correct. . . . I said, 'You guys are absolutely right. Let's work this out so it's doable. What they deserve is much more. But you know my situation.' I told them, 'I just took over a state that is almost bankrupt. So let's work out something that is the minimum we can give those kids and restore their toilets, fix up the roofs that are leaking, the windows that are broken, and create an environment that is a good environment, a safe environment, and also, let's give them the homework material and the books that every other school gets. That is the minimum that we can do.'"

The settlement contradicted Schwarzenegger's stated preference for moving control of the schools from Sacramento to the local districts. But he rationalized it by saying that, in this case, the districts had shown that they were either unable or unwilling to provide equal opportunity to students from low-income families. And the agreement split the difference by giving county superintendents, rather than the state, the power to enforce the new standards.

The $1 billion settlement required the schools to ensure that all students had books and that their campuses were clean and safe. It provided nearly $800 million over four years to make emergency repairs in the lowest-performing schools, about $140 million for new books and other materials, and $50 million for the county officials to assess the schools in their area and oversee the repairs and improvements.

Rosenbaum, the ACLU's legal director in Southern California, called the settlement a "watershed moment" for public education in California. The agreement, he said, would assure "equal educational opportunity" for all children, ending decades of neglect and indifference. He linked it to the landmark 1954 Supreme Court decision, *Brown v. Board of Education*, which ruled school segregation illegal. "Fifty years after Brown," he said, "the dream will no longer be deferred."

That was probably an overstatement. But it was true that Schwarzenegger, a Republican, had taken a major step to improve the education of poor and minority children that his predecessor, a Democrat, had refused to even consider. And it wasn't the last time Schwarzenegger would go down that path.

By the end of his first term, Schwarzenegger had built an intriguing bipartisan record on education issues. He supported programs aimed at helping the poor, which pleased liberals, while defending higher standards, testing, and accountability, which appealed more to conservatives. He supported expanded school choice and he focused on improving vocational education. He opposed raising taxes to pay for preschool for all four-year-olds, but he supported expanding preschool for students in low-income communities.

It was not a program that could be condensed to one or two sentences, like his proposals for infrastructure or health care or global warming. Nor was it an approach that hung together around an articulated theme. Schwarzenegger, after all, had three different education secretaries in his first four years in office. And so his education policy was more of a patchwork of actions and reactions than a well-conceived, unified program.

Its roots, however, were clear: Schwarzenegger's upbringing in Austria and the contrast he saw there with what he saw in America's inner-city schools.

As he kicked off his campaign for governor in 2003, education for poor kids was the one public policy issue with which Schwarzenegger was already identified. That was the mission of his own private foundation. It was also the primary purpose of a ballot initiative, Proposition 49, he had sponsored the year before. That ballot measure proved to be a preview of Schwarzenegger's hybrid approach to problems as the state's chief executive: good motives, imperfect policy, and a fusing of the left and the right to build formidable coalitions that were difficult to stop. Proposition 49, and the experiences that led Schwarzenegger to propose it, also provided an early window into the record the governor would build on public education.

Proposition 49 called for spending up to $550 million per year on after-school programs. The money would go to all schools, but it was targeted first toward schools serving underprivileged kids. And while it dedicated a piece of the state's future revenues to this new priority, the initiative did not raise taxes. It put after-school programs above all other state priorities when new revenues became available, limiting the flexibility of future legislators and governors to set budgets according to their best judgment of the state's needs and its resources. However well intentioned, it was classic ballot box budgeting. It was, in fact, the very kind of auto-pilot spending about which Schwarzenegger would later complain.

As an expansion of a government program aimed at poor children, the proposal found natural backing among liberals. But Schwarzenegger also argued to conservatives that the new spending was an investment that would pay off several times over—in reduced costs for remedial education, and in lower crime rates and lower criminal justice costs, as more kids stayed in school and stayed out of crime. And it could all be done, he noted, without raising taxes.

Campaigning for the measure, Schwarzenegger spoke often about the support he enjoyed as a child. His mother, he said, was always there when he came home from school, and she insisted that he do his homework before going out to play. His father encouraged him to play soccer and participate in other athletic endeavors.

"When I look in those inner-city schools and I see those kids going out after school and not having this kind of supervision, not having this kind of help, not having this kind of love, anyone to help them with their homework, anyone that mentors them and tells them that they're great, I say to myself those kids will never be ready and have the opportunity to use this land that they have, the land of opportunity," Schwarzenegger said in one national television interview. "They will never make it. And so what I promised myself at that point was—is that I'm going to go out and make sure that every child has the same opportunities that I had, and they go out and we'll create more after-school programs, promote after-school programs, and put the spotlight on that issue, and that's what I've been doing for the last 10 years."[5]

Helped in part by his arguments, in part by Schwarzenegger's aura as a celebrity, and in part by a desire among Republican activists to build his image in advance of a run for governor, the measure won the backing of some of California's most powerful interest groups. It was endorsed not only by the California Teachers Association, but also by many of the union's longtime opponents, including the California Taxpayers Association, the Business Roundtable, and the California Chamber of Commerce. It was backed by law enforcement: the California State Sheriffs' Association, the California Firefighters' Association, and the California Narcotics Officers' Association. And it was supported by the Democratic and Republican leaders in the Legislature. It even won the endorsement of the Girl Scout Councils of California and the American Association of Retired Persons. Proposition 49 won easily, with 57 percent of the vote.

Schwarzenegger hoped that his experience passing Proposition 49 would serve as a template for his time as governor, and his settlement of the Williams lawsuit in his first year suggested that a bipartisan approach could work. But his momentum was derailed by major confrontations with the education lobby over money and policy.

Schwarzenegger made two huge early mistakes on education—first by accepting and then by reneging on a budget deal he did not understand. The agreement with the schools lobby saved the state $2 billion in his first year in office as he tried to reduce the deficit he had inherited from his predecessor. But a year later, had he kept to its terms, the deal would have forced him to spend almost every penny of the state's new revenue on the schools, while making deep cuts in health care, welfare, prisons, and higher education. Schwarzenegger never should have made the deal without fully understanding its implications. But once he made it, he should have kept it, or at least done so in the budget he proposed in January 2005. Breaking that promise, and giving voters the impression that he was cutting school budgets even as he was actually increasing them (though not by as much as he had pledged to do) pitted him in a partisan battle with Democrats and the teachers union that undercut everything else he was trying to do.

The first casualties were his poorly chosen and poorly drafted ballot measures in 2005. Putting together a reform package for Schwarzenegger to take to the Legislature, and then to the voters, the governor's advisers insisted that he could not go forward without a proposal on education. But they had nothing prepared on that issue. So they grabbed two ideas, both of which launched him into further conflict with teachers. One called for teachers to work five years instead of two before gaining tenured status. The other proposed that teacher pay be tied to merit rather than years of experience. In addition, a broader budget reform proposal drafted by his team would have amended the state's constitutional guarantee for education funding in a way that made it easier to reduce school funding in bad economic times. Although the merit pay proposal was soon abandoned, the combination of the three amounted to a declaration of war on the teachers and their unions, and it was a war Schwarzenegger would lose.

The result was widespread disenchantment with Schwarzenegger's education policies. Few voters knew about or understood his focus on low-income children, but most had heard about his attempts to slow the growth in spending and his fights with the teachers. And insiders, who were used to governors who led from either the right or the left, but not both, complained that they never knew where Schwarzenegger was coming from.

"This governor talks, then he changes his mind, then he talks, then he changes," Barbara Kerr, the president of the California Teachers Association, said in 2006. "He has no core values whatsoever."[6]

The problem, however, was not that Schwarzenegger lacked core values on education issues. It was that his values did not fit into any previous paradigm for a Republican executive—or for a Democrat, for that matter. Education was his highest priority for new state spending, but he refused to raise taxes to provide as much money as the schools said they needed. He insisted, moreover, that more money was not the only answer, that the schools needed to spend the money they were already getting more effectively. Those sentiments were in line with Republican dogma. But his focus on helping poor kids, on closing the achievement gap between white, affluent children and those from lower-income neighborhoods, was more in sync with the Democrats.

When Schwarzenegger settled another lawsuit—this one filed by the teachers union over his 2005 education budget—he directed nearly $3 billion that was in dispute in that case to about 500 of the lowest-performing schools in the state. Those schools also happened to serve a high number of poor and minority children. Most of the money went toward reducing class size to no more than 25 students per teacher in grades four through eight, and the same ratio was to be maintained in high school for the core subjects of English, social studies, math, and science. High schools that applied for the money would also have to increase the number of counselors so that each one advised no more than 300 students.

Republicans in the Legislature grumbled about the distribution, because little of the money would be going to schools in their districts. Only one Republican in the state Senate, and four in the Assembly, voted for the bill. But the legislation did address traditional Republican calls for more accountability. It required schools getting the extra money to ensure that teachers and administrators were qualified and trained, and it mandated that the schools' teacher corps have at least as much experience as the average in the district. The schools were required to take steps to increase student attendance and graduation rates, and to meet the standards set out earlier in the Williams lawsuit.

Schwarzenegger's record, in fact, was dotted with actions focused on the needs of inner-city kids:

- He signed Senate Bill 1655, which gave principals in low-performing schools the right to refuse to take teachers who were trying to transfer from another campus. The bill was aimed at ending what Schwarzenegger had called the "Dance of the Lemons," whereby bad teachers are shuffled along from one school to another rather than fired. As often as not, they ended their journey at low-performing inner-city schools serving minority children, schools that had frequent openings and had traditionally been forced to accept any district teacher with seniority who applied.

- He gave his support, probably too hastily, to a plan by Los Angeles Mayor Antonio Villaraigosa to take over the Los Angeles Unified School District. Villaraigosa originally wanted to take complete control of the district, but was rebuffed by union leaders, administrators, and officials from other cities served by the district. He finally agreed to a watered-down version of the plan that would have allowed him to take control of three low-performing high schools and the elementary and middle schools that fed them, and to participate with other mayors in hiring new district superintendents and reviewing the district's annual budget. The plan, however, violated the state's constitution, which said no entity other than a school district could be given control over the public schools. It was ruled unconstitutional by two courts before Villaraigosa gave up on it. But by then, Villaraigosa had helped elect a majority to the school board that supported his ideas for reform.

- Schwarzenegger made improving vocational education a big priority, in part to give more options to students who were not going on to college. He added $20 million to the program's budget in 2006 and proposed a bigger increase in 2007. His school construction bond, which voters approved in 2006, included $500 million for new and expanded buildings for "career technical education," as the discipline is now known. And for much of 2007 he traveled the state promoting a renewed focus on offering high-level training to students who were not going on to college.

"We cannot look at that as a second-rate education and the other as a 'higher education,' as we call it," Schwarzenegger said. "This should be treated equally, and that's what our motivation should be, and our goal should be."[7]

• He opposed a 2006 ballot measure to raise taxes on the wealthy to pay for universal preschool in California. Studies showed that most of the money raised by the tax would have gone to subsidize children who already were enrolled in preschool, many of them from middle class or wealthy families. As an alternative, Schwarzenegger proposed and later enacted a program to subsidize expanded preschool for children in neighborhoods where the schools had test scores among the worst 30 percent in the state, schools that were mostly concentrated in poor neighborhoods. That program served about 10,000 children in its first year; a year later, Schwarzenegger proposed to double its size.

• Schwarzenegger stood by the state's system of standards, testing, and accountability, even as some Democrats and the teachers unions tried to weaken it. The system was developed over a decade by two governors from different parties—Republican Pete Wilson and Democrat Gray Davis—and bipartisan votes in the Legislature. The standards spelled out, in great detail, exactly what Californians expected their kids to learn in English, math, science, and social studies, in each grade. The standards were backed by a series of annual standardized tests to assess that knowledge, a system for ranking schools and intervening where students were falling short, and a high school exit exam that every student had to pass to earn a diploma.

Schwarzenegger in 2006 approved $200 million in new education money for more high school counselors, with the condition that schools receiving the money had to develop a specific plan of work for each low-performing 7th grader and every 10th, 11th, and 12th grade student who had not yet passed the exit exam. Schools were also required to schedule counseling sessions with each of those students and their parents. The same budget included an increase of $50 million for tutoring 11th and 12th grade students who had not passed the exam, and $900 million—a 50 percent increase—in special grants to schools that served low-income students and children who were not fluent in English.

In striking that balance—more resources directed at the kids who needed them most, coupled with more accountability— Schwarzenegger was following his instincts. But in doing so, he also found a sweet spot in the electorate. A poll in April 2007 found that 74 percent of all adults agreed that schools in low-income areas should get more money to help pay for teachers and classroom materials. That view was held by 79 percent of Democrats, 73 percent of independents, and 64 percent of Republicans. More than two-thirds of Californians said schools in low-income areas should be able to pay higher salaries to attract better teachers and spend more to train them, even if it cost the state more money.

Other polls also found broad support for the kind of accountability policies that Schwarzenegger supported. By a margin of 72 percent to 26 percent, Californians said they believed students should have to pass a high school exit exam to get a diploma. More than six in ten—64 percent—said they thought teacher pay should be based on merit rather than seniority or years of service. Asked if the schools needed more money or should spend the money they had more wisely, 41 percent of likely voters said the schools should be more efficient, 9 percent said they needed more money, and 49 percent said they should get more money and that they needed to spend it more wisely.

In response to those pressures, Schwarzenegger and the Democratic leaders in the Legislature commissioned a series of academic studies to determine how much money it would take to provide an adequate education to every California child, and what reforms might be necessary to accomplish that goal. The research, paid for by private grants and coordinated by Stanford University, concluded that California would need to increase spending by as much as $60 billion just to raise test scores to state-mandated levels in half the schools. But the research also found that no amount of money would do the job if California did not change the way its schools were run. The report suggested that the state needed to junk an overly centralized, outmoded financing system that emphasized rules over results; adopt new policies to recruit and retain better teachers and administrators while making it easier to fire poor ones; and build a data system that would allow the state, the public, and researchers to track the progress of students from kindergarten through college. Those were the kinds of changes that Democrats, and their allies in the teachers unions, had historically resisted.

After receiving the results of the research, Schwarzenegger and Assembly Speaker Fabian Núñez committed to making 2008 a year of bipartisan education reform in California. "We're going to bring all the stakeholders together, bring both of the parties together, and start hammering away and start talking and dialoguing all the way through until we have come up with solutions," Schwarzenegger said. "Not in a piecemeal way, or not in a fragmented way, but in a big way, and say okay, let's fix all of those things. Let's look at it in a comprehensive way."[8]

It was an ambitious goal, and one that, if achieved, would build on the mostly bipartisan record he had already established on education issues. Rather than continue to tinker around the edges, Schwarzenegger had pledged to enact a fundamental reform of the biggest program in state government, and the one voters valued the most. It would not be an easy task.

FIFTEEN

Mapquest

In his years as a Hollywood megastar, Arnold Schwarzenegger never imagined that he would care so much about the way state legislators and their hired guns drew lines on the political map every 10 years. Like most people, Schwarzenegger hardly knew the process existed, let alone that something insiders called "redistricting" set the course for so much of what happened in politics and government.

But as he absorbed his first detailed briefings on the subject during his campaign for governor in 2003, and later, after he saw the California Legislature up close and personal, Schwarzenegger began to appreciate that the way the lines were drawn helped decide the winners and losers in every district and set the partisan tone for debate in the Capitol.

The drawing of district boundaries is like the DNA of our entire political system. It is complicated, arcane, something few people think about and fewer understand. But those boundaries shape every decision made in all 50 state legislatures and in Congress, influencing the schools our children attend, the roads on which we drive, our health care, our taxes, and our national security.

The issue, moreover, was a perfect fit for Schwarzenegger's independent agenda. The process has historically been tightly controlled by the most partisan figures in the two major parties. It is an insiders' game at which the public is distinctly not welcome. And the way it is done typically contributes to the kind of polarization that independents abhor.

The problem is almost as old as the Republic. The "gerry-mander"—our word for those odd-shaped districts drawn to serve the interests of the politicians and not their constituents—got its name from a plan drawn up for Massachusetts in 1812 and supported by the governor of the commonwealth at that time, Elbridge Gerry. A political cartoonist named one of the lizard-shaped districts after the plan's best-known backer. The label stuck and came to represent the entire genre.

Until about 1980, the process remained fairly crude. The politicians in charge would study election results and voter registration data, note the residences of favored incumbents and those they wanted to get rid of, and then draw districts they hoped would produce the result they desired. If they wanted to protect the reelection prospects of most of those already in power, they drew an "incumbent gerrymander" that packed as many Democrats as possible into Democratic districts and as many Republicans as possible into Republican districts. If the party in power, on the other hand, wanted to extend its majority even further, its line drawers would draw a "partisan gerrymander" that spread the majority party's voters more thinly, creating as many districts as possible that had just enough reliable votes to make them winnable. Either way, there was also plenty of mischief on the side. The line drawers were known to move the boundaries to ensure that an incumbent's mother or largest donor or favorite restaurant was included within his district's boundaries. If two or more legislators who represented adjacent communities were in the leadership's doghouse, those members might be forced into the same district under the new plan so that they would have to run against each other to survive. The whole thing was done with pencil and paper, and as populations grew and shifted over the course of a decade, the effect of the original plan was often diluted.

The computer changed everything. With the advent of digital data, the game grew far more sophisticated. Firms wrote software that allowed the map drawers to easily move individual precincts of a few hundred voters into and out of a district and then instantly test the results in hypothetical elections based on past voting patterns. To these data they added demographics from the census, profiling neighborhoods and districts on the basis of family size, income, and other personal characteristics. This wealth of information proved to be highly accurate in predicting election outcomes, and when combined with information about planned future growth, it allowed the consultants to design districts that not only would be reliable but also would stand the test of time. The districts would carve up counties and cities, cross rivers and even mountain ranges in a search for the right combination of voters. In California, one infamous congressional district had a narrow stretch that ran down the beach for miles so that, at high tide, the district was cut in two.

When Schwarzenegger arrived on the scene, the plan in place in California was an incumbent gerrymander. It had been drawn in 2001 as part of a backroom deal by the national leaders of both major parties, and it was designed to freeze the status quo. Republicans, then in power in Washington, wanted to protect their members of Congress who came from California. Democrats were happy with the edge they already enjoyed in the state's congressional delegation, and they were eager to lock in their big advantage in the Legislature. The resulting deal did both. Republicans got the protection they wanted in Congress. Democrats maintained their lopsided control of the Legislature. In the first 3 elections held using those lines, only 1 seat changed party hands among the 120 seats in the Legislature and 53 in Congress from California.

In a rare moment of clarity, California's Senate leader, Don Perata, acknowledged the way the game worked.

"We are politicians," Perata said, "and we have the interests of incumbents at heart."[1]

But Schwarzenegger never accepted that arrangement. He first addressed the issue during his campaign in 2003, at the urging of Tom McEnery, a respected former mayor of San Jose. McEnery was a lifelong Democrat, the son of a man who had worked in the Truman Administration and been chairman of the California Democratic Party. But coming from the Silicon Valley, where a mix of libertarian economics and social liberalism created an intriguing ideological climate, he had little use for partisan purity and had made redistricting reform something of a life's mission. As the recall campaign got going, he contacted Schwarzenegger through a mutual associate and asked for a meeting.

"I called him up, and I said, 'I want to talk to you about political reform,' and he said, 'Come on down,'" McEnery recalled. "I found him very receptive."[2]

After the meeting in Schwarzenegger's Santa Monica offices, the candidate endorsed the idea of taking the line-drawing power away from the politicians, and the former mayor endorsed Schwarzenegger for governor. The two men soon appeared together at a press conference at the California State Railroad Museum, a location chosen to cast Schwarzenegger as a reformer in the mold of Governor Hiram Johnson, who crusaded against the railroad interests and their control of state politics in the early 1900s.

"Reapportionment of the state Assembly and state Senate seats should be done fairly so that no political party uses the process to distort democracy," Schwarzenegger said at that event.[3]

That same day, Schwarzenegger pledged to strengthen public records laws, ban political fundraising while the state budget was being deliberated, and end the practice of negotiating legislation in secret in the middle of the night. After he was elected, he delegated the public records issue to the Legislature, though he did support a constitutional amendment that modestly improved access to public documents. He hadn't changed the state's fundraising practices by the end of his first term, other than by setting new records—at all times of the year—for fundraising by a governor. And he certainly did not end the habit of cutting deals after midnight. Some of his biggest accomplishments happened in the predawn hours.

But he did keep his promise to pursue redistricting reform, and that promise eventually led to Proposition 77, the measure he endorsed in 2005. The proposal sought to create an independent panel of three retired judges to draw the district lines. The panel was to draw the political boundaries without regard to partisan political data or the residences of incumbents, with the lines required to respect city and county boundaries, as well as geographic barriers and, to protect ethnic minorities, the federal Voting Rights Act.

Although the measure was written by Ted Costa, the Republican gadfly who started the recall movement against former governor Davis, Schwarzenegger helped bring into the fold several prominent Democrats in addition to McEnery. Among them were Leon Panetta, the former Democratic congressman and former chief of staff to President Clinton; Al Checchi, a businessman and Democratic candidate for governor in 1998; former San Francisco mayor Frank Jordan; and Richard Atkinson, the former president of the University of California. Reed Hastings, a Silicon Valley Democrat and founder of NetFlix, the online movie rental business, contributed more than $600,000 to the campaign. The measure was also backed by Common Cause, a respected political watchdog; CalPIRG, a liberal consumer group; and TheRestOfUs.org, a relatively new nonpartisan, Internet-based advocate for political reform. It was endorsed by the *Los Angeles Times*, the *Sacramento Bee*, and the *San Francisco Chronicle*, among others.

Two academic studies of the initiative concluded that it would create more competitive districts in California without giving one party or the other an advantage.

One study, by the Rose Institute at Claremont McKenna College, found that Proposition 77 would likely result in 25 highly competitive districts—up from just 4 that existed at the time the measure was being debated. Ten new competitive districts in Congress would have come at the expense of five safe Democratic seats and five seats that were safe for Republicans. In the Legislature, Democrats might have lost six safe seats, while the Republicans lost five.[4]

A separate study by the Institute of Governmental Studies at the University of California, Berkeley, released after the election, found that the criteria listed in Proposition 77 would have produced from 12 to 14 competitive congressional districts in California. In the 80-member state Assembly, the study found, about 15 seats would have been competitive.[5]

One big reason that reform wouldn't produce even more competitive seats is that more and more, people are choosing to live close to others who share their political views. It is nearly impossible to draw a competitive district in San Francisco, because almost everyone there is a Democrat. The mirror image exists in parts of the Central Valley or Orange County, where Republicans are dominant.

But it does not take very many competitive districts to change the tone and tenor of the government they help produce. When party leaders recruit candidates in safe districts, they usually look for the person, all else being equal, who is most in line with the party dogma. Democratic leaders pick the most liberal candidates and Republican leaders anoint the most conservative. All that those candidates must do is win their party primaries, which tend to be dominated by the most liberal and most conservative voters. Once they have the nomination in a safe district, the general election is a cakewalk because the districts have so few of the other party's voters.

But in a competitive district, just the opposite happens. If a party leader wants to win that seat, he or she must find a candidate whose record and agenda can resonate with independent voters and with voters from the other party. When these candidates take office, they typically vote on process issues with their party leadership but often reach across the aisle to work on substance with the opposition. If there are enough independent-minded members to occupy the balance of power between the ideological purists on both sides, they can play a major role as swing votes in deciding how policy matters turn out.

Schwarzenegger's redistricting proposal was, in short, a bipartisan reform. It is difficult to square the reform's bipartisan nature with the conventional wisdom, then and now, that 2005 was the year in which he was doing the bidding of the national conservative movement. Indeed, more than half of California's Republicans in Congress opposed Schwarzenegger's measure, and the opposition was led by Representative John Doolittle, a lieutenant to then-Majority Leader Tom DeLay and one of the most conservative Republicans in the state's congressional delegation.

"I think people know I am a pretty strong and loyal Republican," Doolittle told the *Sacramento Bee* during the campaign. "This proposition is bad for the Republican Party. . . . The speaker of the House, the entire House leadership, the chairman of the National Republican Congressional Committee and the chairman of the Republican National Committee all think (Proposition 77) is a disastrous idea."[6] Schwarzenegger's proposal, they believed, was nothing less than a threat to the Republicans' margin of power in the House of Representatives.

Republican lawmakers, however, were not alone in their opposition to Proposition 77. Their counterparts on the Democratic side of the aisle were even more opposed. Their plans for taking control of the House rested with an analysis of the status quo, and they did not want to risk their prospects with an independent redistricting. When it came to California, they also had personal political motives. Representative Howard Berman, a Democrat from the San Fernando Valley north of Los Angeles, had long controlled the line-drawing process in California (his brother was a computer geek who did the hands-on work), and he didn't want to give it up. Berman, when he oversaw the drawing of new lines in 2001, had limited the number

of Latinos in his district to guard against a primary challenge. One
of the likely effects of Proposition 77, according to the Claremont
study, would have been to make Berman's district heavily Latino.
That was just one more reason for the powerful congressman to
oppose it.

With both the Republican and Democrat national leadership
against it, Proposition 77 never really had a chance. Hollywood
producer Stephen Bing, a regular contributor to liberal political
causes, donated more than $4 million to the campaign to defeat the
measure. Representative Berman, meanwhile, coordinated fundraising among his congressional colleagues. Most of them donated
at least $25,000 from the campaign committees.

All of this money paid for a highly misleading campaign.
Millions of voters received a full-color brochure telling them that
"powerful forces are trying to rewrite the constitution for their own
political advantage." Proposition 77, the mailing said, was a "political power grab" that would "help one party gain an advantage."
Discerning readers might have noticed that the flyer never said
which party would be gaining the edge. That omission left Democrats to conclude that the measure would help Republicans, while
Republicans were led to believe the opposite. Finally, the mailer
said that the new districts would be drawn by judges "without elections, without any accountability." But Proposition 77 specifically
called for voter approval of the new lines after they were drawn, an
extraordinary level of accountability.

That wasn't all. The opposition campaign also trotted out Judge
Joseph Wapner, once the star of a popular television series called
The People's Court, to complain about the use of retired judges in
the process Proposition 77 would have created. Another ad used
the image of a jigsaw puzzle that, when fitted together, made the
map of Texas. This was a not very thinly veiled reference to the partisan Texas gerrymander engineered by former representative
DeLay. But the California proposal was designed to prevent exactly

the kind of partisan abuse that DeLay and his legislative allies in Texas had put in place to move Democratic districts into the Republican column.

All of this was probably overkill. Given the voters' general unhappiness with the special election and the decline in Schwarzenegger's popularity, all of the governor's measures were headed toward defeat. But the campaign against Proposition 77 did show the lengths to which party leaders would go to hold on to the power to draw new district lines.

In a research paper published after the election by the American Constitution Society, Nicholas Stephanopoulos described Proposition 77 as "likely the highest-profile redistricting initiative ever," but said Schwarzenegger probably never had a chance to succeed.[7] There have been twelve such initiatives in American history, and only four have prevailed, and only two of those victories have come since 1974. Four of the eight failures have come in California. Another came in Ohio on the same day that Schwarzenegger's measure was defeated. In the Buckeye State, though, the politics were reversed, with the Democrats pushing for an independent commission and the Republican Party in full-throated opposition. The only constant was Schwarzenegger: he campaigned for that one too, even though his party opposed it.

"The situation for would-be reformers is dire," Stephanopoulos wrote. "In general, any measure they draft—no matter how well written, no matter how admirable its policy implications—will be defeated. The majority party in the Legislature will rally against the initiative, and reformers will be outspent, outframed, outcampaigned, and, ultimately, outvoted. It matters little whether the governor supports the measure, whether newspapers and interest groups are in favor, or whether the existing electoral districts undermine everything that democracy stands for. The outcome of the campaign will still be the same: failure."

After examining each of the campaigns in detail, Stephanopoulos concluded that the single most important factor in the result was the position of the majority party in the Legislature. If that party was opposed, the measure was almost certain to lose. And while Schwarzenegger lost in 2005, the campaign did lead the state's Democratic leaders—Don Perata in the Senate and Fabian Núñez in the Assembly—to pledge their support for an independent commission, just not the one Schwarzenegger was proposing. And that pledge—if they live up to it—would be the crucial element in determining the success or failure of any future attempt at reform. As of the end of the 2007 legislative session, Perata and Núñez still had not fulfilled their promise to place a new measure on the ballot.

The nation will be watching. If California, which has struggled with this issue more than any other state, can forge a bipartisan consensus to change the way the lines are drawn, then others might follow. Schwarzenegger seems like an ideal spokesman for the cause.

"Arnold has tremendous credibility on this issue," said Ned Wigglesworth of California Common Cause, which has long supported independent redistricting. "He's got the cachet and the delivery skills to make redistricting as relevant as it can possibly be made to people anywhere, in California and across the country. I get the sense he's sincere about it. He gets it. He's not doing it for partisan advantage."[8]

Although the process is complicated, the idea behind reform is simple: Voters should choose the politicians rather than the politicians choosing their voters. That's the message that Schwarzenegger keeps trying to hammer home. If he ever succeeds, he just might leave his state, and the rest of the country, a legacy that would begin to reverse the polarization that has characterized legislative and congressional politics in the twenty-first century.

SIXTEEN

"Get Yourself a Smoking Tent"

Schwarzenegger has never been accused of being modest, and in his second inaugural address, in January 2007, he compared himself to Paul on the road to Damascus. The governor didn't try to argue for sainthood status. But he said that, like Paul, he had undergone a life-changing conversion, in his case a political conversion. Schwarzenegger's bolt of lightning came from California's voters, who rejected all four measures he endorsed on the ballot in November 2005 as he sought to upend the state's political status quo. Looking back more than a year later, Schwarzenegger said he took that sweeping defeat as a signal that the voters wanted him to work for change through consensus, not confrontation.

"I saw that people, not just in California, but across the nation, were hungry for a new kind of politics, a politics that looks beyond the old labels, the old ways, the old arguments," he said. One indication of that yearning was the rise of independent voters, who, he noted, might one day surpass the number of voters registered in either major party.

"They like some of the Republican ideas," he said. "But they also like some of the Democratic ideas. At the same time they think some Republican ideas are too far right. They think some Democratic ideas are too far to the left. And they rightly know that if you stick to just one party's proposals, you miss half of the good ideas."[1]

Schwarzenegger soon hit the road, not for Damascus but for Washington, D.C. There he tried to pitch his notion of "post-partisanship" to the nation's capital, where partisan gridlock had become an art form. Quoting Edmund Burke and JFK on the virtues of compromise, Schwarzenegger lectured the custodians of our national government on their tendency to fight to the death rather than work together toward common goals. Politicians can find middle ground, he maintained, and still be true to their principles.

"The left and the right don't have a monopoly on conscience," he said in a speech at the National Press Club. "We should not let them get away with that. You can be centrist and be principled. You can seek a consensus and retain your convictions. What is more principled than giving up some part of your position to advance the greater good of the people? That is how we arrived at a constitution in this country. Our Founding Fathers would still be meeting at the Holiday Inn in Philadelphia if they hadn't compromised. Why can't our political leaders today?"

He also offered some very specific suggestions.

"In the courtyard of the State Capitol," he said, "I have a politically incorrect smoking tent. People come by, light up a stogie, and schmooze. How come Republicans and Democrats out here don't schmooze with each other? You can't catch a socially transmitted disease by sitting down with people who hold ideas different from yours.

"Someone must start rebuilding trust and relationships in this town. There are very simple ways to begin. To the Democrats, I say stop running down the President, and just tell the people what you would do. To the Republicans, I say stop questioning the motives of the Democrats on the war and accept their right to believe what they want. To the president, I say get yourself a smoking tent. And to all, I would say remember that the majority of people in this country are in the center."[2]

Schwarzenegger's speech drew widespread attention. In some

circles it won him new respect. But in others, it drew only more mockery. Conservative Republicans continued to accuse him of doing little more than caving in to the Democrats who ruled the state's Legislature. And leading Democrats from California did not try very hard to counter that impression. Was Schwarzenegger really doing anything of significance? And even if he was, should it or could it be replicated outside of his own experience, outside of California?

Fabian Núñez, the Democratic speaker of the California Assembly and Schwarzenegger's partner on the global warming legislation, reflected the skepticism about the governor's new mindset when he said that "post-partisanship" meant "we work together on getting stuff done: We do all the legwork. He takes all the credit."[3] But speaking more seriously, Núñez said he thought Schwarzenegger's new approach could be a model for the nation. "What we have been able to do is focus on results, drive an agenda that has an end game attached to it that is a realistic end game, that understands the limitations of both Democrats and Republicans, how far people can go, and builds upon things that you have in common to make gains for the people you represent. Always pushing the envelope more and more, always wanting to get more out of each side. I think that's important."

Schwarzenegger was far from the first major politician to try to build a viable movement in the ideological center. Dwight Eisenhower did it, and his vice president, Richard Nixon, tried the same approach. After the Republicans moved back to the right under the leadership of Ronald Reagan, Bill Clinton found room in the center and seized it with his successful "third way" brand of politics. But as the twenty-first century moved through its first decade, both major parties seemed to be reaching more and more for their ideological bases while ignoring those in the center—and people who, like Schwarzenegger, might hold views that cross party lines.

By the start of his second term, in fact, Schwarzenegger seemed to be the nearest thing in American politics to what author Brink Lindsey calls a "liberaltarian"—a cross between a liberal and a libertarian for which centrist thinkers are increasingly searching. In the *Age of Abundance*, Lindsey argues that the nation's discourse is stuck in a left-right standoff even as the public has moved on, thanks largely to increasing wealth and the spread of technology. He argues that a politician or movement that recognizes a new "libertarian cultural synthesis" could capture the broad center not now occupied by either major party.[4]

> That movement would be "neither anticorporate nor overly chummy with the K Street business lobby; it would maintain a commitment to noninflationary growth; it would support an ample safety net, but one focused on helping (rather than rendering permanently dependent) poor people and people in temporary need, not sloshing money from one part of the middle class to the other (in particular, the elderly); it would oppose corporate welfare; it would endorse vigorous environmental protection while rejecting green Luddism and refusing to accept that the command-and-control regulatory status quo is the final word on the subject; it would shed the left's hostility to law enforcement and middle-class values while insisting that civil liberties and social tolerance are respected; and it would part company with all grand ideological pipe dreams in the realm of foreign affairs (including pacifism as well as neoconservative adventurism), insisting instead that American power is a positive force in the world but one that ought to be used cautiously."[5]

That sounds very much like the approach Schwarzenegger was taking in California. But as Schwarzenegger's experience demonstrates, politicians who try to throw party affiliations overboard and seek consensus solutions to long-standing problems face one big challenge: those solutions tend to lack much of a constituency in the halls of power. If they had strong support from one party or the other, then they wouldn't be in the middle. And while that's exactly where a broad swath of Americans reside, those in the middle are not the ones who control the party organizations or the primaries that produce our politicians.

Jason Kinney, a speechwriter for former governor Davis and now a public affairs consultant in Sacramento, put it succinctly when he assessed Schwarzenegger's dilemma: "This is a guy who can get any world leader, any CEO of any major company, on the phone in two seconds, more so than any other governor in the world," Kinney said of Schwarzenegger. "But the 120 people in the state he has the least influence over are the (members of the) Legislature."[6]

The same could be said of Washington. The national political system has essentially been rigged by partisan activists to favor extremists on both ends. Gerrymandered congressional districts mean that most elections are decided in the party primaries, which are dominated by those with the most ideological passion. Given their power, candidates increasingly speak to those voters, employing a language and a style that turns off the middle even more. Moderate voters are then even less likely to participate, their turnout declines, and the ideological edges grow even more powerful. It is a vicious cycle.

That trend has been aided and abetted by the media. As much as the people who write about politics like to wring their hands at the partisan warfare, they also focus on it, reward it, and encourage it with their stories. Conflict sells. It makes news and draws viewers to television talk shows. Conciliation does not. The game-playing and maneuvering of politics, whether on the campaign trail or inside the capitols, get far more attention than the nuances of policy. Who is up and who is down draws more coverage than what those winners and losers are actually doing or not doing. This may excite partisan junkies who live and breathe politics, but it turns off the people who crave solutions more than scorecards.

Schwarzenegger is trying to empower those people. In 2004 he supported a blanket primary proposal in California that would have allowed all voters to vote in a single primary, with the top two vote-getters, regardless of party, moving on to a general election. But that measure was opposed by both the Democratic and Republican parties, and it lost at the polls. His consistent support for reforming the way political district lines are drawn was also aimed at bringing the middle back to the table. He also supported legislation to move California's presidential primary to the first week of February in order to give the state's voters—and himself—more of a say in selecting the party nominees. Barred as an immigrant from running for president himself, Schwarzenegger met with many of the candidates to encourage them to tackle such issues as global warming, health care, and immigration.

Matthew Dowd, who served as chief campaign strategist to both Bush and Schwarzenegger, says polling shows that a little more than half of American voters are not strongly tied to either major party. Dowd describes these people as true independents plus "Republicans that might believe in big government, or Democrats who believe in small government." Liberal Democrats who believe in a strong and aggressive government amount to only about 23 percent of the national electorate, he says. And "small-government, low-tax, social conservatives" account for only about 25 percent or 26 percent. "The rest of the country," Dowd says, "is in the middle, some mix of things, so those kinds of appeals don't resonate with them."[7]

Will they be strong enough to shift the debate and elect a consensus-builder to the White House?

"I think it's possible," Dowd said. "But I think the portion of the electorate that has so far been passive, that is in the middle, that is tired of it, they're going to have to amplify their voices, which they are beginning to do. And then politicians will tap into it. I don't think the politicians will lead the public there. Politicians will follow a more vocal public who is tired of it and then that change will happen."

In the early stages of the presidential race, the Republicans appeared to be doing more to reach out to the middle than were Democrats, perhaps because Republicans were starting from a position of weakness, given Bush's low approval ratings. Former New York Mayor Rudy Giuliani, who supports abortion rights and gay rights but has conservative stands on economics and foreign policy—a classic independent profile—was an early favorite. Senator John McCain of Arizona, who is more conservative than Giuliani but has worked across party lines in Congress, was also a top contender. Another was Mitt Romney, the former governor of Massachusetts who worked with Democrats to pass the first state legislation requiring residents to carry health insurance. But at the same time, all three of those candidates were courting the Republican base, as any candidate must do if he or she hopes to win a party's nomination. And when none of them were quickly able to nail down the support of the party's right wing, former senator Fred Thompson began planning to enter the race.

The Democrats, whose only two presidents in the last quarter of the twentieth century ran as centrists, appeared set to veer left in reaction to the antipathy party activists felt toward Bush. Senator Hillary Clinton has sometimes governed as a moderate, but, facing intense criticism over her vote in favor of the war in Iraq, she was tacking left on other issues. Senator Barack Obama made some gestures to the center on cultural and family issues, but most of the positions he staked out in the early going could best be described as statist. Former senator John Edwards was running a campaign of envy that tried to pit the poor and the middle class against the wealthy.

If history is any indication, whoever wins the major party nominations will likely move back to the center in the general election in search of independent and moderate votes. But there were some

signs early in the campaign that independents might actually
emerge as a major force even before the general election. In New
Hampshire, which holds the nation's first primary, independents
represented 44 percent of the voters by the spring of 2007, having
doubled their strength since 1992.[8] And since independents in the
Granite State can vote for candidates from either party in the presidential primary, how they break could well determine the winners
in one or both major party races, giving the victors momentum that
could carry them all the way to the nomination. In a perverse cal-
culus, if most of the independents break for a candidate in one of
the parties, that would leave the other party's primary to be dominated by partisans, perhaps propelling the most liberal Democrat
or the most conservative Republican to his or her party nomination. In California, independents will be able to vote in the
Democratic primary but not in the Republican race, giving them a
chance to moderate the Democratic choice while the Republican is
selected by party purists.

A number of groups were working early in the process to try to
organize independents to do more than swing the major party races
in one direction or another. IndependentVoice.org, formed by some
of the remnants of Ross Perot's Reform Party, was trying to connect independents with one another to help them influence the
2008 election. The nonprofit group was loosely affiliated with
IndependentVoting.org, a national umbrella for independent
groups that said it formed to fill a void left by the "reactionary
thrust" of the Republican Party and the "visionlessness" of the
Democrats. That group seemed to be aiming less for the center
than for somehow coalescing independents into something that
would be to the left of the Democrats.

Jim Mangia, the former national secretary of the Reform Party,
said the goal of IndependentVoice.org is to see independent voters
"sway" the political debate rather than simply "swing" in one direction and then another. Independents, he noted, span the ideological

spectrum from very conservative to very liberal, but they share a common disdain for the political system as it stands today. His group is trying to build support for a series of political reforms, including public financing of campaigns, independent redistricting, and open primaries.

"What unifies independents is the belief that there needs to be fundamental change in the way politics is done in the United States," he said. "The stalemate and gridlock of our political system, the failure of either party to deal with problems is what unites independents."[9]

Mangia's group did not plan to create a third party or necessarily support an independent candidate in the 2008 elections. But Unity08 is hoping to do exactly that. That new organization, operating mostly on the Internet, is recruiting delegates, and it plans to nominate a unity ticket of a Republican and a Democrat, or an independent and one major party member in the 2008 presidential election. Unity08 calls itself a "diverse group of Americans who believe that neither of today's parties reflects the aspirations, concerns or will of the majority of Americans. Both parties have polarized and alienated voters. Both are unduly influenced by single-issue groups. Both are excessively dominated by money."

The organization was founded by, among others, Douglas Bailey, a former political consultant and founder of *The Hotline*, a political newsletter, and Gerald Rafshoon, a former media adviser and White House communications director in the administration of President Jimmy Carter. Actor Sam Waterston is promoting the group and its mission.

"If you give moderates a place to rally and a chance to vote for action at the center, the days of divisive politics will be numbered," Waterston said. "We appear to be frozen in the belief that we have no other choice than between a Republican and a Democrat who get to stand for election only by playing to the extremes of their parties and who inevitably compromise themselves because of the cost of running. But we have other options, and if we come across a good one, a carefully conceived one, a constructive and tempered one, we would be foolish not to grab it."[10]

Possible candidates included Angus King, the former independent governor of Maine; Nebraska Senator Chuck Hagel, who has been harshly critical of Bush's conduct of the Iraq war; and New York Mayor Michael Bloomberg, who in early 2007 was considering running as an independent and said he might spend as much as $1 billion to spread his message.

In June, Bloomberg and Schwarzenegger headlined a conference in Los Angeles dubbed "Ceasefire!" in a play on the *Crossfire* cable television talk show that helped define the confrontational, in-your-face style of partisan politics of the era. At the conclusion of the conference, the mayor announced that he was dropping his Republican Party registration and becoming an independent: "We have achieved real progress by overcoming the partisanship that too often puts narrow interests above the common good," Bloomberg said. "As a political independent, I will continue to work with those in all political parties to find common ground, to put partisanship aside and to achieve real solutions to the challenges we face. Any successful elected executive knows that real results are more important than partisan battles and that good ideas should take precedence over rigid adherence to any particular political ideology."

An NBC/*Wall Street Journal* poll in July 2007 found that 53 percent of Americans would favor the creation of an independent party to run a credible candidate for president in 2008. Only 11 percent would not consider voting for an independent. Yet in a three-way matchup of New Yorkers, Clinton was the leading choice in the poll, with 42 percent of the vote, followed by Giuliani with 34 percent and Bloomberg with only 11 percent.

Given his money and his position in New York, it would be foolish to downplay Bloomberg's potential to play a major role in the campaign. But the American system of electing presidents makes it nearly impossible for a third-party or independent candidate to win without one major party or the other completely collapsing. Independent voters and those only loosely aligned with a party might be decisive in choosing a president, but they would have to be almost unanimous in favor of an independent challenger for him or her to win.

Schwarzenegger and Bloomberg have much in common, and they have worked together on some issues. It would not be shocking to see the governor endorse the mayor if Bloomberg ran as an independent and Schwarzenegger was not happy with the other choices.

But beyond any candidate or any election, what Schwarzenegger had in common with all of these groups and potential candidates, and with millions of Americans, was a desire to end the polarization that had paralyzed the nation's politics. That did not mean he was willing to settle for half-measures. To the contrary, he was driven by a desire to do big things. Some of those things were conservative, like reforming the public schools, building more prisons, and making government more efficient. Others had more liberal roots, like expanding access to health care and using government to protect the environment. But as the man in the middle in a rigidly partisan system, Schwarzenegger was nearly alone inside the belly of the beast, and he realized that he could never achieve his goals without help, without changing the way politics worked.

He had gone from bodybuilder to actor to politician, and from consensus-building problem solver to partisan warrior and back again. But by the start of his second term as governor, Schwarzenegger seemed to have found his way. He realized that the loudest voices in the political process were coming from the edges of the debate, and those voices were drowning out the softer tones of mainstream voters. The broad middle that was largely unrepresented needed someone with passion, with energy, and with a flair for the dramatic to carry its message.

He was eager to be that person.

Acknowledgments

This book owes its genesis to Peter Richardson. Shortly after the November 2006 election, Peter asked me if I could explain how Arnold Schwarzenegger won a landslide election as a Republican in a very Democratic state in a very Democratic year, and what Schwarzenegger's victory might tell us about the future of politics in America. I am grateful for Peter's question and his frequent guidance as I tried to answer it, and for his keen attention to detail in the manuscript that resulted.

Peter's curiosity unlocked research and reporting I had been doing since the summer of 2003, when Schwarzenegger first decided to run for governor of California and I began to write about his budding political career. While the conclusions—and any misjudgments or errors—in this book are all mine, I owe a debt to countless others who helped me understand and analyze the governor's campaigns and his time in office, mostly in conversations related to my work with the *Sacramento Bee*. They include his two chiefs of staff, Patricia Clarey and Susan Kennedy; his top campaign advisers, Mike Murphy and Matthew Dowd; his communications directors, Rob Stutzman and Adam Mendelsohn; his former press secretary, Margita Thompson; and his friend and senior adviser, Bonnie Reiss. Several legislative leaders, including senators John Burton, Jim Brulte, Don Perata, Dick Ackerman, and Darrell Steinberg, and Assembly Speaker Fabian Núñez helped explain

Schwarzenegger's relationship with lawmakers along the way. The governor himself has been gracious with his time since 2004, granting me several exclusive interviews, including two lengthy sessions specifically for this book.

I am also thankful for the exhaustive coverage of the Schwarzenegger Administration by my colleagues in the press corps. After the governor's election, a myth developed that, because of his celebrity status, the media were giving him a free ride. Nothing could be further from the truth. I have found the coverage of this governor and his record on policy issues and politics to be more detailed, and in more depth, than the writing about any other chief executive I have followed. Especially noteworthy have been the contributions from Peter Nicholas, Joe Mathews, Dan Morain, and Robert Salladay in the *Los Angeles Times*; Carla Marinucci and Mark Martin in the *San Francisco Chronicle*; Margaret Talev, Gary Delsohn, and Kevin Yamamura in the *Sacramento Bee*; Ed Mendel and John Marelius in the *San Diego Union-Tribune*; and Bill Bradley, an early avid follower of Schwarzenegger's political career, in the *LA Weekly* and, most recently, on the Web with PajamasMedia.com.

Two other sources of information about Schwarzenegger deserve special mention. One is the office of Legislative Analyst Elizabeth Hill. Hill and her staff perform an invaluable function by keeping not only the Legislature but also California's governors honest with their incisive and scrupulously fair analyses of state policies, proposals, and operations. Their critiques of several of Schwarzenegger's policy initiatives were absolutely essential to my understanding of what he was trying to do, what he accomplished, and where he failed. The other is the Public Policy Institute of California, under the direction of president and pollster Mark Baldassare. The Public Policy Institute of California not only provides the best demographic and big-picture policy analysis in

California, it also supplies detailed monthly polling on issues and personalities in state politics. Those polls and Baldassare's interpretation of them gave me an ongoing sense of Schwarzenegger's standing in the state, and the results appear frequently in these pages. I should also note that the Field Poll, while publishing less often, is a California institution that has also provided valuable research on Schwarzenegger and the state's evolving electorate.

When it came time to actually write this book, several people provided assistance without which I would not have been able to complete the task. My editors at the *Sacramento Bee*'s opinion pages, David Holwerk and Maria Henson, supported the project from the start, encouraged me to pursue it with vigor, and were understanding when it sometimes distracted me from my job as a columnist. Maria also was kind enough to read an early draft of the manuscript and suggest changes that ultimately made the final product much better. Robert Salladay read most of the manuscript and served as a sounding board for me throughout the project, to its ultimate benefit. Jenifer Warren reviewed the chapter on state prisons, and her insights improved that section immeasurably.

I also want to acknowledge my dear friends Scott and Vanessa Lindlaw, not only for their comments on the manuscript, but also for helping me find the energy and stamina to write a book while holding down a full-time job as a newspaper columnist. Their inspiration changed my life in ways large and small, and I will be forever grateful to them for it.

I want to thank my father and mother, Jerome and Madeleine Weintraub, for instilling in me an appreciation and interest in the world, in politics, and in civic affairs, and for their lifelong and unconditional support of my career in journalism. I have told them too rarely how much their love and affection has meant to me.

But none of the contributions mentioned above would have mattered without the love, support, and companionship of my wife of 25 years, Janice Selby. Her enthusiasm, her courage, and her incredible work ethic, both on the job and in our home, enabled me to pursue my career and to devote as much time and attention as I needed to this project with the knowledge and comfort that she would always be there when I needed her. No man could ask for anything more.

Notes

CHAPTER 1: BOOTSTRAPS

1. Transcript available at www.freeto choose.net/1990_vol1 _transcript.html.

2. Interview with the author, March 30, 2007.

3. Interview with the author, April 4, 2007.

4. Interview with the author, March 30, 2007.

5. Speech to "Perspectives" conference, Sacramento, September 21, 2001; available at www.schwarzenegger.com/en/life/hiswords/ words_en_sac_perspectives.asp?sec=life&subsec=hiswords.

6. Interview with the author, March 30, 2007.

7. "Perspectives" speech.

8. I was not the first to use this phrase to describe Schwarzenegger. As far as I know, Joe Mathews and Peter Nicholas of the *Los Angeles Times* were the first to put it into print.

CHAPTER 2: A STATE OF CONFUSION

1. Natural gas prices nearly doubled between January 2000 and the end of May, from $2.40 per million Btu to $4, according to the U.S. Energy Information Administration. By December, the price was $10.

2. The NASDAQ closed at 5048.62 that day. A little more than two years later, on October 9, 2002, the index had fallen to 1114.11.

3. "Dynamics of the Silicon Valley Economy," Public Policy Institute of California, October 2004. Available at www.ppic.org/content/pubs/jtf/JTF_SiliconValleyJTF.pdf.

4. All of these tax and income figures are from the California Franchise Tax Board.

5. Interview with the author. Starr's quotes first appeared in a column I wrote for the *Sacramento Bee*, published on August 31, 2003.

CHAPTER 3: FIVE HUNDRED PUSH-UPS

1. Interview with the author, March 30, 2007.

2. Joe Mathews, *The People's Machine: Arnold Schwarzenegger and the Rise of Blockbuster Democracy* (Cambridge, Massachusetts: Public Affairs, 2006), p. 151.

3. Interview with the author, April 24, 2007.

4. Interview with the author. Tamminen's quotes were first published in a column I wrote for the *Sacramento Bee* on October 16, 2005.

5. Interview with the author; first published in the *Sacramento Bee* on October 16, 2005.

6. Betsy Streisand, "It's crunch time for the California budget mess as Governor Schwarzenegger tries to cut some deals," *U.S. News and World Report*, January 12, 2004.

7. Betsy Morris, "Arnold power," *Fortune Magazine*, August 9, 2004, p. 76.

8. Interview with the author. Panetta's quote was first published in a column I wrote for the *Sacramento Bee* on October 16, 2005.

9. Interview with the author, March 30, 2007.

10. Interview with the author, April 25, 2007.

CHAPTER 4: FUSION

1. August 6, 2003, CNN *Breaking News* transcript.

2. I believe that journalist Bill Bradley, then of the *LA Weekly*, was the first to describe Schwarzenegger in print as a "fusion" Republican. See "True Lies," *LA Weekly*, August 14, 2003, p. 23.

3. From author's transcript of the event.

4. John Gittelsohn, "The campaigner," *Orange County Register*, November 16, 2003.

5. *Los Angeles Times* exit poll, March 2, 2004.

6. Steve Geissinger, "Governor lauds deficit bond win," *Oakland Tribune*, March 3, 2004.

7. State budget summary, Schedule 6, January 2007.

8. Author's calculations, based on numbers from the Department of Finance, Legislative Analyst.

9. May 14, 2007, press conference; transcript supplied by the Office of the Governor.

CHAPTER 5: TAKING CARE OF BUSINESS

1. Interview of Lawrence Higby with the author. Higby's comments were first published in a column I wrote for the *Sacramento Bee* on October 8, 2003.

2. Steve Lawrence, "Schwarzenegger on pace to become California's biggest-ever fundraiser," *Associated Press*, November 4, 2006.

3. Peter Nicholas and Dan Morain, "Governor's aides got big bonuses for political work," *Los Angeles Times*, January 20, 2007.

4. Marisa Lagos, "Schwarzenegger: No quid pro quo for donors," *San Francisco Chronicle*, October 11, 2006.

5. Gilbert Chan, "Bending a bit on workers' comp," *Sacramento Bee*, March 25, 2004.

6. Public Policy Institute of California, Special Survey of Los Angeles, March 2004.

7. Transcript supplied by the Office of the Governor.

8. Mark Martin, "Changes sought in rules on lunch breaks," *San Francisco Chronicle*, December 15, 2004.

CHAPTER 6: YEAR OF REFORM

1. *NBC News* transcript, July 19, 2004.

2. Peter Nicholas, "Gov. criticizes legislators as 'girlie men,'" *Los Angeles Times*, July 18, 2004.

3. Interview with the author. Kaufman's quote first appeared in a column I wrote for the *Sacramento Bee* on November 13, 2005.

4. Gary Delsohn, "Governor calls GOP to 'Great Battle,'" *Sacramento Bee*, February 12, 2005.

5. Secretary of State documents and article by Steve Lawrence, Associated Press, February 2, 2006.

6. Mark Z. Barabak, "Reluctant warrior bests Gov.," *Los Angeles Times*, November 10, 2005.

CHAPTER 7: LESSONS LEARNED

1. Transcript of Schwarzenegger press conference in the Capitol, November 10, 2005. Office of the Governor.

2. Transcript of Schwarzenegger press conference in the Capitol, November 10, 2005. Office of the Governor.

3. Governor's interview with George Stephanopoulos, *ABC News*, January 14, 2007.

4. Interview with the author, June 19, 2007.

5. Gary Delsohn, "Governor's pick likely a Democrat," *Sacramento Bee*, November 30, 2005.

6. Interview with the author, June 19, 2007.

7. Angelides campaign kickoff in Sacramento, March 15, 2005. The author was present.

CHAPTER 8: CRANES

1. John Marelius and Philip J. LaVelle, *San Diego Union-Tribune*, August 19, 2006.

2. Interview with the author. Kennedy's quote first appeared in a column I wrote for the *Sacramento Bee*, November 12, 2006.

3. Lynda Gledhill, *San Francisco Chronicle*, January 10, 2006.

4. Perata made these comments in an interview in February 2006. with the *Sacramento Bee*'s editorial board. They were first published in a column by the author on February 14, 2006.

5. Harrison Sheppard, "New try in failed bond bid," *Daily News of Los Angeles*, March 17, 2006.

6. Statement from Westly for Governor campaign, March 16, 2006.

7. Feinstein's statement was distributed by the Rebuilding California coalition on October 20, 2006.

8. Press conference in Santa Monica, November 8, 2006. Transcript provided by the Office of the Governor.

CHAPTER 9: JOLLY GREEN GOVERNOR

1. Carla Marinucci, "Recall spotlight on Appeals Court," *San Francisco Chronicle*, September 22, 2003; and Laura Mecoy, "Schwarzenegger says jobs, environment can be protected," *Sacramento Bee*, September 22, 2003.

2. Andy Bowers, "Gore versus the Governator," *Slate Magazine*, May 3, 2007.

3. Interview with the author, March 30, 2007.

4. Interview with the author, April 6, 2007.

5. Terry Tamminen, *Lives per Gallon: The True Cost of Our Oil Addiction* (Washington, D.C.: Island Press, 2006), pp. 45–46.

6. "Green Building Action Plan," December 14, 2004.

7. Mark Martin, "Governor acts to curb state's gas emissions," *San Francisco Chronicle*, June 2, 2005.

8. "Schwarzenegger mixed record on display at Treasure Island," California League of Conservation Voters, September 27, 2006.

9. Joint letter to Senate Leader Don Perata, August 24, 2005.

CHAPTER 10: THE RISE OF THE INDEPENDENT VOTER

1. Interview with the author, March 30, 2007.

2. Interview with the author, May 27, 2007.

3. Raymond Wolfinger, Bruce E. Keith, David B. Magleby, Candace J. Nelson, Elizabeth Orr, and Marc C. Westlye, *The Myth of the Independent Voter* (Berkeley and Los Angeles: University of California Press, 1992).

4. Bill Cavala, "Too dumb to choose," CaliforniaProgress Report.com, June 5, 2006.

5. *Los Angeles Times* exit poll, October 7, 2003.

6. www.TheModerateVoice.com.

7. Interview with the author, May 31, 2007.

8. Interview with the author, June 19, 2007.

CHAPTER 11: TO YOUR HEALTH

1. Interview with the author, May 17, 2007.

2. Interview with the author, May 17, 2007.

3. Harrison Sheppard and Mike Zapler, "Semantics debate plagues governor's health care plan," *Contra Costa Times*, January 14, 2007.

4. Kevin Yamamura, "Governor tries to get enemies into his tent," *Sacramento Bee*, January 14, 2007.

5. California State Employees Association report on rally, May 8, 2007.

6. Press conference at the state Capitol with the governor and legislative leaders, May 10, 2007. Transcript from the Office of the Governor.

CHAPTER 12: "I AM AN IMMIGRANT"

1. Bill Bradley, "Collateral Damage," *LA Weekly*, August 22, 2003. Bradley wrote that in 2002, "while campaigning for Proposition 49, his after-school programs initiative, Schwarzenegger won a standing ovation from the Commonwealth Club at the Fairmont Hotel in San Francisco, when he responded to a question from the audience about his current thinking on Prop. 187: 'I would never stand in the way of any child going to school, whether he or she is here legally or illegally, it does not matter.'"

2. Assembly Bill 1463 in 2000.

3. Assembly Bill 60 in 2002.

4. *Fox News* broadcast, "The O'Reilly Factor," September 10, 2003.

5. KFMB radio in San Diego, *The Rick Roberts Show*, February 2, 2004.

6. Carla Marinucci, "Close the borders, Schwarzenegger says," *San Francisco Chronicle*, April 20, 2005.

7. Carla Marinucci, "Schwarzenegger apologizes for 'Close the borders' remark," *San Francisco Chronicle*, April 21, 2005.

8. John Marelius, "Governor's kudos for Minutemen brings outcry," *San Diego Union Tribune*, April 29, 2005.

9. Carla Marinucci and Mark Martin, "Governor endorses Minutemen on border," *San Francisco Chronicle*, April 29, 2005.

10. Daniel Weintraub, "Big issue, big governor, big mystery," *Sacramento Bee*, April 2, 2006.

11. Margaret Talev, "Schwarzenegger details views," *Sacramento Bee*, September 7, 2003.

CHAPTER 13: JUSTICE DELAYED

1. Andy Furillo, "Report: Prison reform derailed," *Sacramento Bee*, June 22, 2006.

2. State of the State speech to the Legislature, January 9, 2007. Transcript from the Office of the Governor.

3. The measure was known as Assembly Bill 900.

4. Andy Furillo, "Capital embraces prison deal—but will judges?" *Sacramento Bee*, April 27, 2007.

5. Perata speech on the Senate floor, April 26, 2007.

6. Conference call with California newspaper editorial writers, May 3, 2007.

7. Conference call with California newspaper editorial writers, May 3, 2007.

CHAPTER 14: GOING TO SCHOOL

1. Associated Press report, May 20, 2000.

2. Nanette Asimov, "Davis feels heat over student depositions," *San Francisco Chronicle*, September 6, 2001.

3. Interview with the author, May 17, 2007.

4. Interview with the author, July 25, 2007.

5. Schwarzenegger interview with Chris Matthews, MSNBC, October 29, 2004.

6. Dana Hull, "Teachers union president slams Schwarzenegger over 'core values,'" *San Jose Mercury News*, February 26, 2006.

7. Ed Mendel, "Governor puts spotlight on career technical education," *San Diego Union Tribune*, May 6, 2007.

8. Press conference in the Capitol, March 14, 2007. Transcript from the Office of the Governor.

CHAPTER 15: MAPQUEST

1. Perata said this at a town hall meeting in Walnut Creek during the campaign over Schwarzenegger's ballot measures, October 24, 2005.

2. Interview with the author. McEnery's comments were first published in a column I wrote for the *Sacramento Bee* on October 20, 2005.

3. Sandy Kleffman, "Schwarzenegger reveals campaign reform plan," *Contra Costa Times*, September 19, 2003.

4. "Restoring the competitive edge: California's need for redistricting reform and the likely impact of Proposition 77," the Rose Institute of State and Local Government, September 26, 2005.

5. "Competition and redistricting in California: Lessons for reform," Institute of Governmental Studies, UC Berkeley, February 7, 2006.

6. David Whitney, "Doolittle opposes proposition on redistricting, but activists, other Republicans, back it," *Sacramento Bee*, September 11, 2005.

7. Nicholas Stephanopoulos, "Reforming redistricting: Why popular initiatives to establish redistricting commissions succeed or fail," *American Constitution Society for Law and Policy*, March 6, 2007. Available at www.acslaw.org/node/4414.

8. Interview with the author, April 19, 2007.

CHAPTER 16: "GET YOURSELF A SMOKING TENT"

1. Schwarzenegger's second inaugural speech, January 5, 2007. Transcript of the speech from the Governor's 2007 Inaugural Committee.

2. Transcript of the speech as prepared, from the Office of the Governor.

3. Interview with the author, May 2, 2007.

4. Brink Lindsey, *The Age of Abundance: How Prosperity Transformed America's Politics and Culture* (New York: HarperCollins Publishers, 2007).

5. Brink Lindsey, *The Age of Abundance*, p. 336.

6. Panel discussion on postpartisanship, Great Valley Center annual conference, Sacramento, May 10, 2007.

7. Interview with the author, June 19, 2007.

8. David Shribman, RealClearPolitics.com, May 5, 2007.

9. Interview with the author, May 29, 2007.

10. Speech to the National Press Club, April 25, 2007. Transcribed by the author from video at Yahoo Videos. http://video.yahoo.com/video/play?vid=476106&fr=

Index

About the Author

Daniel Weintraub is a native Californian who was born and raised in San Diego County, the youngest of eight children who spanned the Baby Boom. He graduated in economics from San Diego State University and began his career in journalism writing for the *Los Angeles Times* in San Diego. He covered California's Capitol for the *Times* for eight years before becoming Capitol Bureau Chief and columnist for the *Orange County Register*. Since 2000, he has been the public affairs columnist for the opinion pages of the *Sacramento Bee*, where he writes about the intersection of politics and public policy. He lives in Sacramento with his wife, Janice. They have two sons, Max and Abe.

Other Books from PoliPointPress

The Blue Pages: A Directory of Companies Rated by Their Politics and Practices   Helps consumers match their buying decisions with their political values by listing the political contributions and business practices of over 1,000 companies. $9.95, paperback.

Jeff Cohen, *Cable News Confidential: My Misadventures in Corporate Media*   Offers a fast-paced romp through the three major cable news channels—Fox CNN, and MSNBC—and delivers a serious message about their failure to cover the most urgent issues of the day. $14.95, paperback.

Marjorie Cohn, *Cowboy Republic: Six Ways the Bush Gang Has Defied the Law*   Shows how the executive branch under President Bush has systematically defied the law instead of enforcing it. $14.95, paperback.

Joe Conason, *The Raw Deal: How the Bush Republicans Plan to Destroy Social Security and the Legacy of the New Deal*   Reveals the well-financed and determined effort to undo the Social Security Act and other New Deal programs. $11.00, paperback.

Kevin Danaher, Shannon Biggs, and Jason Mark, *Building the Green Economy: Success Stories from the Grassroots*   Shows how community groups, families, and individual citizens have protected their food and water, cleaned up their neighborhoods, and strengthened their local economies. $16.00, paperback.

Reese Erlich, *The Iran Agenda: The Real Story of U.S. Policy and the Middle East Crisis*   Explores the turbulent recent history between the two countries and how it has led to a showdown over nuclear technology. $14.95, paperback.

Steven Hill, *10 Steps to Repair American Democracy*   Identifies the key problems with American democracy, especially election practices, and proposes ten specific reforms to reinvigorate it. $11.00, paperback.

Yvonne Latty, *In Conflict: Iraq War Veterans Speak Out on Duty, Loss, and the Fight to Stay Alive*   Features the unheard voices, extraordinary experiences, and personal photographs of a broad mix of Iraq War veterans, including Congressman Patrick Murphy, Tammy Duckworth, Kelly Daugherty, and Camilo Mejia. $24.00, hardcover.

Phillip Longman, *Best Care Anywhere: Why VA Health Care Is Better Than Yours*   Shows how the turnaround at the long-maligned VA hospitals provides a blueprint for salvaging America's expensive but troubled health care system. $14.95, paperback.

Christine Pelosi, *Campaign Boot Camp: Basic Training for Future Leaders*   Offers a seven-step guide for successful campaigns and causes at all levels of government. $15.95, paperback.

William Rivers Pitt, *House of Ill Repute: Reflections on War, Lies, and America's Ravaged Reputation*   Skewers the Bush Administration for its reckless invasions, warrantless wiretaps, lethally incompetent response to Hurricane Katrina, and other scandals and blunders. $16.00, paperback.

Nomi Prins, *Jacked: How "Conservatives" Are Picking Your Pocket— Whether You Voted For Them or Not*   Describes how the "conservative" agenda has affected your wallet, skewed national priorities, and diminished America—but not the American spirit. $12.00, paperback.

Norman Solomon, *Made Love, Got War: Close Encounters with America's Warfare State*   Traces five decades of American militarism and the media's all-too-frequent failure to challenge it. $24.95, hardcover.

John Sperling et al., *The Great Divide: Retro vs. Metro America*   Explains how and why our nation is so bitterly divided into what the authors call Retro and Metro America. $19.95, paperback.

Curtis White, *The Spirit of Disobedience: Resisting the Charms of Fake Politics, Mindless Consumption, and the Culture of Total Work*   Debunks the notion that liberalism has no need for spirituality and describes a "middle way" through our red state/blue state political impasse. Includes three powerful interviews with John DeGraaf, James Howard Kunstler, and Michael Ableman. $24.00, hardcover.

For more information, please visit www.p3books.com.

About This Book

This book is printed on Cascade Envir0100 Print paper. It contains 100 percent post-consumer fiber and is certified EcoLogo, Processed Chlorine Free, and FSC Recycled. For each ton used instead of virgin paper, we:

- Save the equivalent of 17 trees
- Reduce air emissions by 2,098 pounds
- Reduce solid waste by 1,081 pounds
- Reduce the water used by 10,196 gallons
- Reduce suspended particles in the water by 6.9 pounds.

This paper is manufactured using biogas energy, reducing natural gas consumption by 2,748 cubic feet per ton of paper produced.

The book's printer, Malloy Incorporated, works with paper mills that are environmentally responsible, that do not source fiber from endangered forests, and that are third-party certified. Malloy prints with soy and vegetable based inks, and over 98 percent of the solid material they discard is recycled. Their water emissions are entirely safe for disposal into their municipal sanitary sewer system, and they work with the Michigan Department of Environmental Quality to ensure that their air emissions meet all environmental standards.

The Michigan Department of Environmental Quality has recognized Malloy as a Great Printer for their compliance with environmental regulations, written environmental policy, pollution prevention efforts, and pledge to share best practices with other printers. Their county Department of Planning and Environment has designated them a Waste Knot Partner for their waste prevention and recycling programs.